Betty Crocker's
LOW-FAT,
LOW-CHOLESTEROL
COOKBOOK

....

Betty Crocker's
LOW-FAT,
LOW-CHOLESTEROL
COOKBOOK

....

**PRENTICE
HALL
PRESS**

....

New York • London • Toronto • Sydney • Tokyo • Singapore

PRENTICE HALL PRESS
15 Columbus Circle
New York. NY 10023

PRENTICE HALL PRESS and colophons are registered trademarks
of Simon & Schuster. Inc.

BETTY CROCKER is a registered trademark
of General Mills. Inc.

Library of Congress Cataloging-in-Publication Data

Crocker. Betty.
   [Low-fat. Low-Cholesterol Cookbook]
   Betty Crocker's low fat. low cholesterol cookbook.
     p.   cm.
   ISBN 0-13-084484-5 : $18.95 (est.)
    1. Low-fat diet—Recipes.   2. Low-cholesterol diet—Recipes.
I. Title.
RM237.C76   1991
641.5'638—dc20   90-30968
                                          CIP

Manufactured in the United States of America

10 9 8 7 6 5 4 3 2 1

First Edition

Page 2:

An abundance of delicious, nutritious low-fat foods.
On the cover: Chicken Breasts with Sun-dried-tomato Sauce
(page 78)

CONTENTS

....

INTRODUCTION

· ·

Today's interest in healthful living is more than a passing fancy. People have been calorie-conscious for years, but it is only recently that the importance of *what* we eat has prevailed over that of *how much* we eat. The roles fat and cholesterol play in coronary heart disease, we now understand, are significant ones. It is clear that managing a healthful diet means making informed choices about how much fat we eat.

Can "sensible" food be enjoyable? Cooking scrumptious low-fat, low-cholesterol food is probably easier than you imagine, and this book is full of tips and techniques that will make gradual changes toward more healthful eating simple and fun. One hundred eighty-five delicious recipes offer lots of variety, while making the most of produce at its freshest and brightest. Twelve terrific menus make putting together meals—not to mention parties—a snap, and menu plans for two full days emphasize the importance of the "bigger picture."

Experts recommend that no more than 30 percent of our daily calorie intake come from fat. It is easy to figure how many of your daily calories are fat calories; just follow the steps explained on page 22.

With the help of this book, you will learn how to adjust your own favorite recipes to be lower in fat and cholesterol, too. And the dividend is this: Great-tasting recipes mean you can indulge in delicious, good-for-you food while enjoying a more healthful life-style. There are simple changes we can make in our lives, changes that make a difference in how well we feel and in how we enjoy ourselves. Reducing the amounts of fat and cholesterol in our diets is one of them. If only all those changes were this easy and delicious!

—THE BETTY CROCKER EDITORS

Tandoori Chicken with Raita (page 82), Tropical Fruit Cream Pie (page 186)

Chapter 1

Here's to Your Health

Good health, a long life, happiness—three goals many of us share. Characteristic of the path to those goals is a healthful life-style. And although what a healthful life-style means to each individual may differ somewhat, there are some common themes there, too.

Healthful eating and exercise habits are extremely important in the pursuit of a healthful life-style. In the following pages, we'll explore just what healthful eating is all about and look briefly at the importance of regular exercise. You may be surprised to learn that pleasure can be part of a healthful life-style and, in fact, is vital to it!

Cutting Down on Fat and Cholesterol

One overriding dietary concern today is the amount of fat we eat. High blood cholesterol is a major risk factor for coronary heart disease (CHD), our nation's number one killer. And more than any other dietary factor, saturated fat in the diet can raise our blood cholesterol levels. Less fat, however, means fewer calories—an extra incentive to keep our fat intake down.

According to the National Institutes of Health (NIH), more than 50 percent of all adult Americans have blood cholesterol levels higher than "desirable." Half of these people have levels that are considered "high."

Currently, almost 38 percent of the calories in the average American diet comes from fat. This represents about 75 grams of total fat in a typical 1,800-calorie daily diet. Seventy-five grams of fat would be, for example, about 5⅓ tablespoons or ⅓ cup of solid margarine per day. The

---

Risk Factors for Coronary Heart Disease

High blood cholesterol
High blood pressure
Family history of coronary heart disease before the age of 55
Cigarette smoking

Diabetes
Vascular disease
Obesity
Being male
Sedentary life-style

TOTAL SERUM CHOLESTEROL CLASSIFICATION

DESIRABLE SERUM CHOLESTEROL	BORDERLINE-HIGH SERUM CHOLESTEROL	HIGH SERUM CHOLESTEROL
Below 200 mg/dl	200–239 mg/dl	240 mg/dl and above

LDL CHOLESTEROL CLASSIFICATION

DESIRABLE	BORDERLINE-HIGH RISK	HIGH RISK
Less than 130 mg/dl	130–150 mg/dl	160 mg/dl and above

HDL CHOLESTEROL CLASSIFICATION

DESIRABLE
Above 35 mg/dl

Source: *Report of the Expert Panel on Detection, Evaluation and Treatment of High Blood Cholesterol in Adults*, National Cholesterol Education Program, National Heart, Lung and Blood Institute, U.S. Dept. of Health and Human Services, NIH Publication 88-2926, 1987.

Tex-Mex Scrambled Eggs (page 118)

American Heart Association (AHA) and many other health organizations recommend that healthy adults reduce their total fat intake to less than 30 percent of daily calories (about sixty grams in an 1,800-calorie diet); that's easy to calculate, as you can see on page 22.

In addition to the problem of high fat intake, our dietary cholesterol levels are higher than they should be. Average cholesterol intake now stands at 350 to 400 milligrams daily. Health experts suggest we limit daily intake to less than 300 milligrams of cholesterol.

What many of us don't realize, however, is that we need some fat. You may be interested to know that fat and cholesterol play very positive roles in good health.

What Is Fat?

Fats are made up of carbon, hydrogen and oxygen atoms. The different kinds of fats are distinguished by differences in their chemical structure.

Sources of Fat

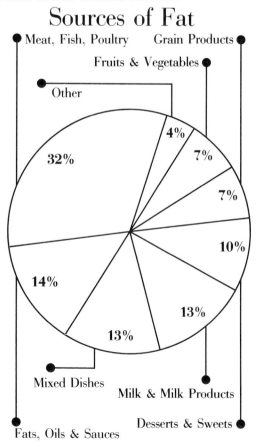

Source: General Mills, Inc., Diet Study, General Mills, Inc., 1983–1985.

The building blocks of fat are fatty acids. Fatty acids are saturated, monounsaturated or polyunsaturated. We'll talk more about these later.

Over the last forty years, we've cut down on our intake of fat from animal sources. Today we're eating more vegetable fats in the form of salad dressings and oils. The greatest amount of fat in the average American diet, however, still comes from meat, fish and poultry. Looking at the pie chart below in the left column you can see how fat contributes to our daily diets.

Fat does help keep us healthy, though, in several ways because it:

♦ *Provides linoleic acid, a fatty acid essential to proper growth, healthy skin and metabolism of cholesterol.*

♦ *Helps transport, absorb and store the fat-soluble vitamins A, D, E and K.*

♦ *Insulates and cushions body organs.*

♦ *Supplies energy. It's the most concentrated source of calories (nine calories per gram of fat versus four calories per gram for protein and carbohydrate).*

♦ *Satisfies us. Because it takes longer to digest, fat stays with us longer, helping to control hunger. What's more, it tastes good!*

Saturated Versus Unsaturated Fats

Saturated fats are solid at room temperature and are found mainly in animal sources. Foods that contain higher amounts of saturated fats include meats, eggs and dairy products (whole milk, hard cheese, butter and cream). Tropical fats—coconut, palm and palm kernel oils—are unique because they come from plants, yet they too contain significant amounts of saturated fats.

Scientific evidence demonstrates a link between a diet high in saturated fats and the incidence of high blood cholesterol. All saturated fats, however, do not have the same cholesterol-raising potential. (Research conducted on palm oil, which is high in saturated fatty acids, indicates that it behaves differently from other saturated fats. Why these differences exist is not clear, and more research is needed to study the long-term effects of these fatty acids on blood cholesterol levels.)

Fats and oils that contain mainly unsaturated fatty acids are liquid at room temperature and are found most commonly in plant sources. Substituting these fats for saturated fats may help to lower blood cholesterol levels. Olive oil and peanut oil are high in *mono*unsaturated fats while corn, soybean, safflower and sunflower oils contain considerable amounts of *poly*unsaturated fats.

All foods that contain dietary fat are actually made up of mixtures of saturated and unsaturated (*mono*-unsaturated and/or *poly*unsaturated) fatty acids. In fact, even dietary fats such as cooking oils and margarine contain a mixture of these types of fatty acids. For example, 49 percent of the fat in butter is saturated while 31 percent is unsaturated. Olive oil, well known for its *mono*unsaturated fat, which makes up 73 percent of the total fatty acid content, is a better choice, even though it also includes 13 percent saturated fat. You'll want to choose fats that contain more unsaturated fat than saturated fat. But the level of saturation of any fat can be altered by a process called hydrogenation.

What Is a Hydrogenated Fat?

Hydrogenation is a way to change unsaturated fatty acids to have a more saturated chemical structure. This is accomplished by adding more hydrogen to the fatty acid molecule. Highly unsaturated vegetable oils are not stable enough for use in packaged foods because they develop "off flavors" in short periods of time. To increase stability or "shelf life," some alteration such as hydrogenation of the oil is often necessary. Shortening made by blending hydrogenated vegetable oils, like coconut or palm oil, can improve flavor and extend the shelf life of packaged foods. When hydrogenated,

vegetable oil margarine becomes solid and spreadable at room temperature, and when refrigerated properly, it maintains an acceptable flavor.

Another category of fats, called "omega-3 fatty acids," is unique. These are highly polyunsaturated fatty acids found in fish, shellfish and plants from the sea. As a general rule, the higher the fat content of the seafood, the more omega-3 fatty acids it contains.

Research suggests that diets rich in omega-3 fatty acids may help reduce the risk of heart disease. Many health organizations recommend that we eat more fish and shellfish.

What Is Cholesterol?

Essential to life, cholesterol is produced by the body. In fact, the body makes 800 to 1,500 milligrams of cholesterol each day, which circulates through the bloodstream. Cholesterol has important functions in the body. It helps to produce certain hormones and is a vital part of your nervous system and brain.

A soft, waxy, fatlike substance, cholesterol is found *only* in animal foods. That means plant foods—grains, fruits, vegetables, nuts—do *not* contain cholesterol. The cholesterol in the foods we eat is *dietary* cholesterol, while the cholesterol in our *blood* comes from two sources—the foods we eat and the body's own manufacturing process. For most people, dietary cholesterol has only a small influence on blood cholesterol because the body controls the level in the bloodstream. Even so, health experts recommend that we limit the dietary cholesterol from our foods to 300 milligrams each day. The easiest way to do that is to learn which foods contain cholesterol.

The most concentrated sources of *dietary* cholesterol are organ meats, such as liver, brain and kidney. Egg yolk also contains a significant amount. The table on the following pages lists the cholesterol content of some familiar foods. Compare the different foods so you'll know the better choices.

Fat and Cholesterol Content of Selected Foods

FOOD	MEASURE UNIT, WEIGHT	TOTAL FAT, G	CHOLESTEROL, MG
Whole milk	1 cup	8.9	35
Skim milk	1 cup	0.4	4
Plain yogurt	6 ounces	5.5	21
Plain nonfat yogurt	6 ounces	0	5
Whipped heavy cream	2 tablespoons	1.3	4
Prepared whipped topping mix, prepared with whole milk	2 tablespoons	1.0	trace
Vanilla ice cream, 16% fat	1 cup	23.7	88
Vanilla ice milk	1 cup	5.6	18
Sour cream	1 cup	48.2	102
Lowfat sour cream	1 cup	28.8	96
Creamed cottage cheese	1 cup	9.5	31
Lowfat cottage cheese	1 cup	4.4	19
Ricotta cheese, whole milk	15 ounces	54.8	216
Lowfat ricotta cheese, skim	15 ounces	33.6	131
Cream cheese	1 ounce	9.9	31
Neufchâtel cheese	1 ounce	6.6	22
Cheddar cheese	1 ounce	9.0	30
Lowfat Cheddar cheese	1 ounce	5.0	20
Swiss cheese	1 ounce	8.0	25
Lowfat Swiss cheese	1 ounce	5.0	20
Lard	1 tablespoon	12.8	12
Butter	1 tablespoon	11.5	31
Margarine, corn	1 tablespoon	11.5	0
Reduced-calorie margarine	1 tablespoon	8.0	0
Eggs	1 large	5.1	217
Cholesterol-free egg product	¼ cup	0	0
Vegetable oil, corn	1 tablespoon	13.6	0
Nonstick cooking spray	1 spray	1.0	0

FOOD	MEASURE UNIT, WEIGHT	TOTAL FAT, G	CHOLESTEROL, MG
Mayonnaise, soybean	1 tablespoon	11.0	8
Cholesterol-free reduced-calorie mayonnaise	1 tablespoon	5.0	0
Italian salad dressing	1 tablespoon, bottled	8.0	0
Reduced-calorie Italian salad dressing	1 tablespoon, bottled	0	0
Blue cheese salad dressing	1 tablespoon, bottled	6.0	0
Reduced-calorie blue cheese salad dressing	1 tablespoon, bottled	2.0	0
Egg noodles	2 ounces, dry	3.0	70
Cholesterol-free noodles	2 ounces, dry	1.0	0
Tuna, oil packed, drained	3 ounces, canned	6.9	26
Tuna, water packed, drained	3 ounces, canned	2.1	35
Salmon, Chinook	3 ounces, baked	11.0	69
Flounder, sole	3 ounces, baked	1.3	58
Crab legs	3 ounces, cooked	1.0	45
Imitation crabmeat sticks	3 ounces, cooked	1.1	17
Ground beef	3 ounces, broiled	17.6	76
Extra-lean ground beef	3 ounces, broiled	13.9	71
Beef boneless rib roast	3 ounces, roasted	8.0	65
Beef top round steak	3 ounces, broiled	6.0	72
Pork shoulder blade steak	3 ounces, braised	14.0	83
Pork loin tenderloin	3 ounces, roasted	4.0	79
Chicken, dark meat without skin	3 ounces, roasted	8.3	79
Chicken, light meat without skin	3 ounces, roasted	3.8	72
Turkey, dark meat without skin	3 ounces, roasted	6.1	72
Turkey, white meat without skin	3 ounces, roasted	2.7	59
White layer cake with white frosting	¹⁄₁₂ slice	14.0	0
White angel food cake, unfrosted	¹⁄₁₂ slice	0	0

Sources: Compiled by General Mills, Inc. from U.S. Department of Agriculture Handbook #8, Michigan State University data base, Egg Board, product labels and manufacturer information.

What are HDLs and LDLs?

Here is what happens to dietary cholesterol once it gets into the bloodstream. Substances called low-density lipoproteins (LDLs) carry cholesterol from the liver (where it is formed) to cells throughout the body. Excess cholesterol is deposited on artery walls. These deposits or "plaques" can build up over time and can contribute to CHD (coronary heart disease). Other blood-cholesterol carriers called high-density lipoproteins (HDLs) carry excess cholesterol away from the artery walls and back to the liver for reprocessing or removal from the body. HDLs help to prevent cholesterol build-up.

For some people, it may not be enough just to know their total blood cholesterol number. This is especially true for people whose total blood cholesterol is 240 milligrams per deciliter of blood or higher. A blood profile can determine the levels of LDLs and HDLs. This type of analysis may be advisable for those with borderline–high cholesterol levels (200 to 239 milligrams per deciliter) plus two risk factors for CHD (for example, smoking and high blood pressure) or for people who already have CHD. Look at the chart on page 9 and make note of your CHD risk factors. A desirable LDL level is less than 130 milligrams per deciliter while a desirable HDL level is above 35 milligrams per deciliter of blood.

A direct relationship exists between the total blood cholesterol level and the level of LDL. Three known causes of elevated LDL and blood cholesterol levels are:

- *Genetic factors and family history*
- *A diet high in saturated fats and cholesterol*
- *Health conditions, such as diabetes, diseases of the liver and kidney or an underactive thyroid*

A low level of HDL may indicate an increased risk of heart disease. Some possible causes of low HDL levels include lack of exercise, obesity, smoking and high blood cholesterol and/or triglycerides (another type of fat in the blood).

The next step is learning how to use all this information about fat and cholesterol to change your eating habits.

Reducing Fat in Your Diet

Physicians, nutritionists and researchers have developed some guides to help you reduce the amount of fat and cholesterol you eat.

- Eat fewer high-fat foods. Eating less *visible* fat like lard, shortening or oil is important, but *hidden* fat is abundant too. Limiting fat intake may mean eating less ice cream, fewer chips and less of creamy or cheesy mixed dishes. We need to be aware of the fat in food—its type and quantity—to make choices that will keep total fat intake and calories down.

- Eat smaller portions. Remember, just because a food is high in fat or cholesterol doesn't mean we can't eat it at all. It just means we should eat smaller servings, less often.

- Choose cooking methods that use less fat. Broil, bake, roast, grill, poach, steam, stew and microwave foods whenever possible. You can stir-fry, too, if you use small amounts of unsaturated oils.

- Use nonstick cookware. A nonstick skillet and one or two nonstick saucepans with a nonstick-cooking spray can easily lessen the amounts of fat used in cooking.

- Serve chicken, turkey or fish often. Light-meat chicken and turkey are naturally low in fat, especially if you remove the skin. Most fish is also very lean. Even such higher-fat fish as salmon are as lean or leaner than poultry and lean beef. Some fish also have the added benefit of omega-3 fatty acids.

- Choose lean cuts of meat and trim fat. There are many leaner cuts of beef, pork and lamb now widely available. Trim visible fat before cooking. (It's probably not a good idea to completely eliminate meats from the diet because they are important sources of many other nutrients, among them iron and vitamin B_{12}, that may be hard to get from other foods.)

- Use lowfat or skim milk products. Many milk products contain a great deal of fat, especially if they are made with whole milk or cream. Choose from the many lowfat and nonfat dairy products that are available. Look for skim milk, lowfat or skim milk cheeses and lowfat or nonfat yogurt. Don't eliminate dairy products entirely, because they provide the calcium needed for healthy bones.

◆ Limit added fats and oils to five to eight teaspoons per day. We're talking about how much butter you add to bread and the amount of dressing or mayonnaise you load on salads. Try reduced-fat margarine and dressings. Remember, there's no need to give up fats completely. But we do need to be aware of how much we eat and limit portions or make substitutions wherever possible.

◆ Limit eggs to four per week. With 217 milligrams of cholesterol, one egg yolk supplies more than two-thirds the recommended daily limit. The good news is that egg whites have no cholesterol and in many cases can be used instead of whole eggs. Try omelets made with one whole egg and four egg whites, or use an egg substitute. Look for recipes that allow for these substitutions.

◆ Substitute complex carbohydrates for foods high in saturated fat and cholesterol. Complex carbohydrate is another term for starch and fiber. Once thought of as fattening, starch now has gained new glory as a low-fat energy source. No need to skimp on pasta, cereals and rice. The potatoes we once shunned are now invited to our tables. Other sources of complex carbohydrates are breads, vegetables and fruits. Just go easy on the margarine, mayonnaise and creamy sauces.

Speaking of complex carbohydrates, read on for more about fiber.

Bulking Up with Roughage

Although generations of grandmothers have long known the value of roughage in the diet, scientific interest in fiber has increased only in recent years.

Fiber began to make a comeback in the 1960s, when Dr. Denis Burkitt reported that rural Africans had diets consisting of foods with more fiber than did people in industrialized civilizations. Africans had a lower incidence of cancer of the colon (large intestine) than did Americans or Europeans. Diverticulitis of the colon walls, some forms of heart disease, diabetes and other diseases all occurred with much less frequency in the African group.

Since the turn of the century, the amount of fiber in American diets has declined. As new information emerges about the link between health and fiber, experts are recommending that we increase our intake. Fiber consumption is now "in style."

Fiber is part of the structure of plants. It is found in many foods containing complex carbohydrates, such as whole-grain cereals and breads and many vegetables and fruits. Fiber is not found in meat or dairy products. According to scientists, *dietary* fiber is the nondigestible material that remains after plant foods pass through the intestinal tract. It is not a single substance but a complex mixture of many. Not all dietary fiber is alike.

Total dietary fiber can be divided into two types— *soluble* and *insoluble* fiber. Soluble fiber, as its name suggests, dissolves in water. Insoluble fiber, what Grandma called roughage, does not dissolve in water. Some of the most important information to develop from recent research is the difference between these two kinds of fiber.

Insoluble fiber promotes regularity and is being studied for its potential to reduce risks of colon and rectal cancers. But until recently, soluble fiber was practically ignored, largely because its role was unclear. Some important effects of soluble fiber on the digestive and absorptive processes have been demonstrated, and soluble fiber may help to lower blood cholesterol when part of a low-fat diet. Soluble fiber shows promise in helping to control blood sugar levels in some diabetics, too. See page 212 for a list of good sources of soluble and insoluble fiber.

Many people are confused about the relationship of bran to dietary fiber. Bran is the coarse, outer layer of the whole-grain kernel; this layer is the major source of fiber in the grain. In addition to fiber, bran contains some starch, protein, vitamins, minerals and a small amount of fat. But all brans are not created equal. Depending on the grain source of the bran, it will contain different amounts of soluble and insoluble fiber.

Currently, there are no established Recommended Dietary Allowances (RDAs) for fiber although some health associations suggest that we eat twenty-five to thirty-five grams of total dietary fiber each day. Translated into food choices, that means:

◆ *Four or more servings of fruit and vegetables.*

◆ *Four or more servings of breads, cereals and legumes (pears and beans). Choose whole-grain varieties of breads and cereals several times a day.*

Putting It All Together

Fat, cholesterol and fiber are only three considerations for a healthful diet. We need more than forty different nutrients for good health, so even when we understand the facts about good nutrition, it may seem we need to be experts to come up with a sound plan. Fortunately, that work has already been done for us.

Back in the 1940s, we began to realize more fully the potential impact of diet on our health. Emerging from the Depression era when people regularly experienced food shortages, we saw a great number of people with diseases related to deficiencies of certain nutrients. To combat this national health problem, nutritionists devised a plan for daily eating that divided foods into groups according to similarity in nutrient content.

The *Bread/Cereal/Grain Group* provides carbohydrate, iron and B vitamins (thiamin, riboflavin and niacin). Servings from the Bread/Cereal/Grain Group include one ounce of breakfast cereal, one slice of bread, three crackers and ½ cup cooked cereal. Everyone needs *four or more servings* of these foods daily.

The *Fruit/Vegetable Group* is made up of just that— all fruits and vegetables. This group gives us carbohydrate and vitamins A and C. One whole piece of fruit or ½ cup cooked vegetables or ½ cup of canned fruit are some examples of servings. Eat at least *four servings* from this group each day.

Iron, protein, niacin, vitamin B_6 and vitamin B_{12} (from animal sources only) come from the *Meat/Poultry/ Fish/ Alternatives Group*. *Two servings* daily are enough for everyone. A serving of these is two or three ounces of lean protein (beef, poultry, fish), one egg, two tablespoons of peanut butter or ½ cup of cooked legumes (peas and beans).

Eat *two servings* from the *Dairy Group* each day. This group gives us the calcium, phosphorus, protein and vitamins A and D we need. One serving includes 1½ ounces of cheese, one cup of milk or eight ounces of yogurt. Pregnant women or those who are breast-feeding should consume three servings. Children, too, need three servings daily and teens require four.

The Fats/Sweets/Alchohol Group provides fatty acids and vitamin E. But avoid too much from this group, especially if you're trying to lose a few pounds.

By eating the recommended number of servings daily from the food groups listed, you can ensure you will meet your needs for the many essential nutrients. Keep in mind, however, the dietary considerations listed at the beginning of this chapter. When the food groups were first devised, nutrient *deficiencies* were a concern. Today, we're more likely to be getting too much of certain nutrients, rather than too little.

Remember to consider the content of fat, cholesterol, starch and fiber of each food. Also, think about how much salt or sodium, sugar, calcium and iron you eat. We discuss these issues in the following pages.

Other Important Nutrients

Protein plays a role in many body processes and is vital to growth and maintaining and repairing body tissues. In addition to the foods you commonly think of as "protein" foods, such as meats, cheese and eggs, protein is found in breads, cereals, beans and peas. In the United States, we tend to eat more than twice the amount of protein we need, and experts think we should eat less. By limiting the number of servings and portion sizes to those we talked about earlier, you'll meet the recommendation.

You may have heard a lot about *calcium* because of its role in maintaining strong, healthy bones and teeth. Osteoporosis, a condition whereby bones become porous and brittle, threatens great numbers of older women in our country today. Along with several other factors, calcium deficiency may be a factor in the development of osteoporosis. There's speculation, too, that high blood pressure may result from too little calcium. Adolescent girls and adult women should be particularly careful to eat foods high in calcium. Dairy foods such as milk, cheese and yogurt are very good sources, although calcium is also found in dark green leafy vegetables, such as broccoli and collard greens, and in fish with edible bones, such as canned salmon and sardines.

In some people, too much *salt* (sodium chloride) and *sodium* may contribute to the development of high blood pressure. Although it's impossible to predict who will develop high blood pressure, and not everyone who does is affected by the amount of salt they eat, it's wise to keep sodium intake to a moderate level. Current U.S. averages estimate we eat 4,500 milligrams of sodium daily. However, we should try to reduce our daily intake to about 3,300 milligrams. One way to do that is to use less salt at the table and in food preparation and only eat high-sodium foods occasionally. A diet without added salt and that doesn't include high-sodium foods averages about 2,000 milligrams of sodium daily. That's just less than one teaspoon of salt (about 2,300 milligrams of sodium). And besides helping to control blood pressure, sodium is needed for proper kidney, nerve and muscle function.

Another nutrient, *iron*, is necessary for oxygen transfer to body cells and, therefore, plays a vital role in how much energy we have. Iron-deficiency anemia (a disease from not enough iron) continues to be a health problem in the United States, particularly among women of childbearing age who lose iron monthly through menstruation. Children, adolescents and members of low-income families are at high risk for iron deficiency also. Iron is getting even more attention lately as people eat less red meat in the interest of health. Choosing lean meats, however, can see to it that you get enough iron and still keep your fat intake in line. Other good sources of iron include dried beans and peas, iron-enriched cereals and whole-grain products.

Sugar's reputation as a dietary "bad guy" is generally undeserved. The only health problem that sugar has been linked to is the development of dental cavities. And for those who are particularly vulnerable to cavities, especially children, limiting how much sugar they eat and how often they eat it is important. But it isn't only sugar; any carbohydrate food can cause tooth decay—even crackers or fruit—if you're not brushing properly. Brushing after meals and snacks helps to cleanse teeth by removing cavity-forming bacteria. However, if high-sugar sweets are eaten to the exclusion of more nutrient-rich choices, it is wise to cut back.

Choosing Healthy Foods

As the American life-style continues to quicken in pace and fewer people take time to prepare homemade foods, it becomes increasingly important to be able to read and understand the information food manufacturers provide about the nutritional content of their products. Once we learn how to read labels, we are better able to make informed food choices.

At present, not all foods are required to carry a *nutrition label*. Only those food products that have added nutrients or make a nutrition claim on the label or in advertising (such as, "low cholesterol" or "sodium free") are required by law to do so. All other foods, except those with standards of identity (see below), are required to list ingredients on the label in descending order of predominance by weight.

For example, the *ingredient list* on a regular can of green beans might read, "Green beans, water, salt." This means that the can contains more green beans than water or salt, and more water than salt. If, however, the green beans are labeled "low salt," a nutrition information panel must be featured on the label. The information that must appear on the panel is currently undergoing review, but the illustration on page 209 highlights what you can expect to find.

Foods with *standards of identity* are not required to contain an ingredient list. These foods must include a specified list of ingredients, which is on file at the United States Food and Drug Administration, in order to be called by a specific name. If additional ingredients are used, however, they must be listed on the label. Foods with standards of identity include ketchup, mayonnaise, peanut butter, jam and other common foods. (These guidelines are currently under review, and will change somewhat in both content and format by the mid-1990s.)

Balancing Pleasure and Good Nutrition

While proper nutrition is vital to good health, let's not forget the pleasurable role that food plays in our lives. It may seem unfortunate that many of our favorite foods are high in fat, salt or sugar. Even so, in the context of a total diet, there's plenty of room to continue to enjoy these foods while eating healthfully. The bottom line is variety, balance and moderation— the basics of good nutrition.

Choosing a wide variety of foods helps to ensure that we're getting all of the nutrients we need, while avoiding an excess of any one of them. Variety also helps to satisfy our taste buds through a wide choice of different foods with differing flavors.

In light of our food concerns today, balance helps us keep fat, cholesterol, salt and sugar in line with current recommendations. Simply put, balance means alternately choosing foods low in fat, cholesterol, salt or sugar. "Perfect" foods aren't practical or necessary. What's important is how food choices balance throughout the day.

Moderation focuses on both the amount of food you eat and the frequency with which you eat certain foods. Read food labels to learn recommended portion sizes of different foods. Then, remember, it's not necessary to give up any foods completely. Just reduce the amount you eat and the frequency to keep the fun in a healthful diet.

Exercise—Vital to a Healthful Life-style

What you eat is just one aspect of a healthful life-style. Many other factors also play a role. Among those factors, exercise takes a lead. A program of regular exercise can help you achieve or maintain a healthful body weight, reduced blood pressure and increased HDL levels. Regular exercise can help you maximize your potential for good health. It doesn't have to be a tedious chore, either!

Contrary to our nation's previous obsession with such high-intensity exercises as jogging, recent research indicates that moderate exercise can be very beneficial. Walking, playing golf and even housecleaning help firm muscles and burn extra calories.

Getting started is most often the difficult part of exercising. The following ideas can help you get past that crucial start-up point.

◆ Choose activities that you enjoy.
◆ Vary exercises to avoid boredom and to fit with the season. Try swimming in summer and cross-country skiing in winter so you can enjoy the outdoors while keeping fit.
◆ Make a list of activities you can do alone or with family and friends. Flexibility helps you stay with your exercise program.

◆ Alternate aerobic activities with weight-bearing and flexibility exercises to take care of your fitness needs. Walking and running fill two bills in that they are both weight-bearing and can be aerobic. Vigorous bike riding and swimming are other aerobic exercises. Stretching exercises increase flexibility.
◆ Plan ahead to fit exercise into your schedule. If you leave it as a last-minute decision, you may never find the time.
◆ Choose a time that blends easily into your schedule so exercise becomes a regular routine.

Go Slowly for Greater Success

With eating habits or exercise, it's important to realize the value of gradual change. You've spent a lifetime developing your current habits, and if you expect to change all of them overnight, you may be undermining your chances for success. Try to take on one or two challenges at a time and allow time to adjust. Small changes that add up to new overall habits are often the best way to guarantee success. Start by identifying major problem areas in your eating and exercise routines. Then prioritize those problems to determine which ones to tackle first.

Plan strategies that will help you overcome your hurdles. For example, if you eat too many high-fat foods and too few fruits, vegetables and complex carbohydrates, resolve to eat carrot sticks, red pepper rings, cherry tomatoes or broccoli flowerettes instead of chips with your noontime sandwich. Change your standard breakfast to skim milk, cereal and fruit instead of eggs and bacon. Cut back on the amount of meat you eat by preparing meals that are combinations of vegetables, meat and complex carbohydrates such as mixed rice or pasta dishes. Remember, there's no need to completely forgo your less-healthful food favorites. You can continue to eat these foods occasionally.

Once you have control over the problem areas at the top of your list, move on to other areas that you think need improvement. If, even after reducing the amount of fat in your diet, you find that you're still eating a bit too much and consequently weigh more than you'd like to, work to reduce your portion sizes. Or, if regular exercise is a problem for you, focus on increasing your activity level, thereby burning up those extra calories.

To make health a part of your life-style, a commonsense blend of pleasure and good judgment may be the best approach. That way, you'll move closer to all three of the goals we spoke of at the beginning of this chapter—good health, a long life and happiness. To help you get started, here are a dozen menus, designed for any occasion.

Low-fat, Low-cholesterol Menus

FAMILY FAVORITES

Herbed Pot Roast (page 46)
Mixed green salad with Creamy Herb Dressing (page 160)
Sour Cream Biscuits (page 142)
Rice Pudding (page 188)

CELEBRATE IN STYLE

Apple slices and water crackers with Coeur à la Crème (page 31)
Dijon Veal Roast (page 55)
Sweet Potato-Apple Puree (page 150)
Broccoli with Cheese Sauce (page 166)
Warm Greens with Balsamic Vinaigrette (page 160)
Blueberry-Lime Torte (page 193)

BY THE HEARTH

Crackers with Chutney-glazed Yogurt Spread (page 35)
Spicy Black Bean and Pork Stew (page 68)
Two-Pear Waldorf Salad (page 158)
Easy Multigrain Bread (page 149)
Pineapple Bread Pudding with Rum Sauce (page 189)

COMPANY'S COMING

Breadsticks with Caponata (page 31)
Savory Fish en Papillote (page 97)
Saucy Jerusalem Artichokes (page 154)
Spinach Salad with Raspberry-Peppercorn Dressing (page 163)
Parmesan-Pepper Rolls (page 145)
Chocolate Swirl Cheesecake with Raspberry Topping (page 194)

TWO BY TWO

Chicken Terrine (page 43) with Spinach-Herb Sauce (page 167)
Glazed Cornish Hens with Plums (page 89)
Leeks au Gratin (page 154)
Individual Cranberry-Orange Desserts (page 191)

FIESTA FLAIR

Bell Pepper Nachos (page 36)
Southwest Fajitas (page 49)
Chili-Corn Pudding (page 153)
Mixed green salad with Chipotle Dressing (page 162)
Strawberry Margarita Pie (page 185)

VEGETARIAN LUNCHEON

Vegetable Frittata (page 43)
Wheat Berry Salad (page 139)
Zucchini-Apricot Bread (page 148)
Lemon Meringue Cake with Strawberries (page 181)

TEENS TAKE OVER

Guacamole (page 28) with Spicy Tortilla Chips (page 39)
Whole Wheat Ratatouille Calzone (page 131)
Zesty Fruit Salad (page 157)
Vanilla ice milk with Chocolate Sauce (page 199)
Chocolate Chip Cookies (page 203)

AT THE PARK

Tarragon Stuffed Eggs (page 39)
Sesame Chicken Salad (page 87)
Carrot sticks
Basil–Red Pepper Muffins (page 144)
Peppermint Brownies (page 199)

BACKYARD BARBECUE

Vegetable dippers with Green Herb Dip (page 28)
Gingered Flank Steak (page 46)
Two-Potato Salad with Dill Dressing (page 159)
Corn-on-the-cob
Frosted Banana Bars (page 201)

A BUNCH FOR BRUNCH

Mushroom and Leek Quiche (page 122)
Potato-Basil Scramble (page 119)
Citrus-Currant Scones (page 144)
Pumpkin-Fruit Bread (page 148)
Fruit cups
Spicy Plum Cake (page 177)

THE EVENING CROWD

Black Bean Dip (page 30) with pita chips
Crackers with Bell Pepper Spread (page 35)
Stuffed Pattypan Squash (page 40)
Chicken Satay (page 37)
Chinese Firecrackers (page 40)
Lemon-Ginger Trifle with Apricots (page 192)
Creamy Peach Freeze (page 198)

From the menu, "By the Hearth" (clockwise from top): Two-Pear Waldorf Salad (page 158), Easy Multigrain Bread (page 149), Pineapple Bread Pudding with Rum Sauce (page 189), Spicy Black Bean and Pork Stew (page 68)

Planning Your Day

It is a good idea to know approximately how much of your daily caloric intake comes from fat. You can figure the percentage of fat in your daily diet very easily. First, add the total number of calories consumed. Add up, separately, the number of grams of fat consumed. Multiply the number of grams of fat by nine (there are nine calories per gram of fat) for a total number of fat calories. Now, divide the number of fat calories by the total number of calories. That will give you a fraction, which you can think of as a percent by multiplying by 100—the percent of calories that come from fat.

The two full-day menu plans that follow show you examples of how to calculate the fat in a day's worth of meals. Each of the following menu plans builds a full day's meals for you. Nutrition profiles have been calculated for each day using the equation above to figure the amount of calories from fat. Remember to choose no more than 30 percent fat daily. As you can see from these plans, each day is well below that, yet neither is short of good food to eat.

FAMILY FAVORITES MENU PLAN

Breakfast

1 cup unsweetened strawberries
1 Spicy Apple-Bran Muffin (page 145) with 1 tablespoon Neufchâtel cheese
1 cup skim milk
Coffee or tea

Lunch

1 serving Chicken-Vegetable Soup (page 87)
1 slice Easy Multigrain Bread (page 149) with 1
 teaspoon margarine
1 cup skim milk
1 medium orange

Dinner

1 serving Herbed Pot Roast (page 46)
1 serving Tangy Carrots with Grapes (page 149)
Mixed green salad with 1 tablespoon Creamy Herb
 Dressing (page 160)
12 ounces sparkling water
1 serving Rice Pudding (page 188)

Snacks

1 medium carrot
2 Italian Biscotti (page 207)

Calories	1,685	Fat	42 g
Protein	98 g	Unsaturated	32 g
Carbohydrate	235 g	Saturated	10 g
Sodium	2,280 mg	Cholesterol	190 mg

Percent fat calculation (using equation explained above, left):

42 g fat $\times$ 9 calories/g = 378 calories

$$\frac{378 \text{ calories}}{1,685 \text{ calories}} = 0.224$$

0.224 $\times$ 100 = 22.4 = 22 percent calories from fat

BACKYARD BARBECUE MENU PLAN

Breakfast

½ medium grapefruit
3 Whole Wheat Blueberry Waffles (page 142) with 3
    tablespoons reduced-calorie maple-flavored syrup
1 cup skim milk
Coffee or tea

Lunch

1 Bean Patty (page 135)
Mixed green salad with 1 tablespoon reduced-calorie
    Italian dressing
1 cup skim milk
1 medium pear

Dinner

Vegetable dippers with 2 tablespoons Green Herb
    Dip (page 28)
1 serving Gingered Flank Steak (page 46)
1 serving Two-Potato Salad with Dill Dressing
    (page 159)
1 ear corn-on-the-cob with cracked pepper
12 ounces light beer
1 Frosted Banana Bar (page 201)

Snacks

1 medium apple
1 cup Southwestern Popcorn Snack (page 36)

Calories	2,055	Fat	44 g
Protein	106 g	Unsaturated	32 g
Carbohydrate	300 g	Saturated	12 g
Sodium	2,550 mg	Cholesterol	160 mg

Percent fat calculation (using equation explained on page
22):

44 g fat × 9 calories/g = 396 calories

$$\frac{396 \text{ calories}}{2,055 \text{ calories}} = 0.193$$

0.193 × 100 = 19.3 = 19 percent calories from fat

Feast on Your Favorites

Reducing the amount of fat and cholesterol in your diet does not mean that you must eliminate all of your favorite recipes from your current repertoire. Simply review your recipes and reduce the amounts of ingredients high in fat or replace them with low-fat and low-cholesterol alternatives. Virtually all dairy products are available today in low-fat versions, as are many other products and ingredients.

Decreasing your fat intake doesn't have to be an abrupt change. If you drink whole milk, switch to 2 percent milk. A few months later, move to 1 percent milk, then to skim milk. If you make changes gradually, it is easier to adapt to changes in flavor.

Substitute one of the commercial cholesterol-free egg products available, or make your own Egg Substitute from our recipe on page 116. Often you can leave out egg yolks and just use the whites in place of whole eggs; many baked goods can be made without yolks while most custards require at least some yolk. Refer to the substitution chart on page 212 for amounts. A drop or two of yellow food color will give recipes made with egg whites the appearance of having been made with whole eggs.

Reduce cholesterol by using margarine or an unsaturated oil instead of butter in cooking and baking. In many recipes, the oil, shortening or margarine for sautéing onions, garlic or chopped vegetables can be omitted. Invest in a nonstick skillet and add nonstick cooking spray, water, broth, herb vinegar or wine instead of the fat. The White Sauce on page 166 shows you how to reduce fat drastically; it's made with only half the margarine of a traditional white sauce and further reduces fat and cholesterol with skim milk rather than whole milk.

Baking is a little trickier. When lowering fat in your favorite recipes, make only small alterations until you achieve the product you want. Start by replacing the egg yolks with whites. Decrease the shortening to the next even measurement. If a recipe calls for ½ cup margarine, try ⅓ cup; if that works well, go on to ¼ cup the next time. It is unlikely that the shortening can be decreased by more than one-half and still give you good results. Ten bread recipes, beginning on page 142, and baking recipes throughout "Delicious Desserts" will help get you started.

Reduce the amount of such fatty additions as nuts, olives, cheese and chocolate in your recipes and grate or chop them into smaller pieces so they will distribute more evenly. A small amount of miniature chocolate chips in both the Chocolate Chip Cookies (page 203) and the Coco-Oatmeal Cookies (page 203) works very nicely. Although nuts contain no cholesterol, they are high in fat, so reduce amounts or leave them out of most recipes.

The recipes in this book were not developed to be low in sodium, but only enough salt was added to bring out flavor. You can do the same with your own recipes. Don't add salt to recipes containing high-sodium ingredients. For example, Three-Cheese Noodle Bake (page 128) is made with three cheeses, which all contain quite a bit of sodium; no additional salt is needed. When a recipe calls for several ingredients high in sodium, use a low-sodium version of one of them when possible. We used no-salt-added tomato paste in the Oriental Barbecued Chicken (page 76) to balance the sodium in the hoisin sauce. Just get in the habit of using the low-sodium version of such products as soy sauce.

Altering a recipe to be lower in fat can be as simple as using nonfat yogurt for regular yogurt and Neufchâtel cheese for cream cheese, as we have done in the Coeur à la Crème recipe that follows. This simple adjustment saves twenty calories, three grams of fat and nine milligrams of cholesterol per tablespoon.

To prepare our low-fat, low-cholesterol version of Coeur à la Crème, please turn to page 31.

Coeur à la Crème

2 cups plain yogurt **NONFAT**
1 package (8 ounces) ~~cream~~ cheese, softened **NEUFCHÂTEL**
2 tablespoons chopped fresh or 2 teaspoons dried dill weed
2 tablespoons chopped fresh or 2 teaspoons dried chervil
2 tablespoons chopped fresh parsley
½ teaspoon salt
½ teaspoon pepper

Line 3-cup mold with holes in bottom or 6-inch strainer with double-thickness cheesecloth or single paper coffee filter. Place mold in dish. Beat yogurt and cheese in medium bowl on medium speed until smooth. Stir in remaining ingredients. Mound mixture in mold. Cover mold and dish and refrigerate at least 24 hours. Unmold onto serving plate. Serve with cucumber slices and crackers if desired.

Nutrition for original version Coeur à la Crème:

About 2¼ cups spread

Per tablespoon:			
Calories	30	Fat	3 g
Protein	1 g	Unsaturated	1 g
Carbohydrate	1 g	Saturated	2 g
Sodium	55 mg	Cholesterol	10 mg

Nutrition for low-fat version Coeur à la Crème:

About 2¼ cups spread

Per tablespoon:			
Calories	20	Fat	2 g
Protein	1 g	Unsaturated	1 g
Carbohydrate	1 g	Saturated	<1 g
Sodium	65 mg	Cholesterol	5 mg

When you are comfortable making substitutions with low-fat ingredients, look at whole components of recipes that can be altered. We have made some major changes in the following Mushroom and Leek Quiche, while still maintaining the original concept of the recipe. A traditional pastry crust has about ⅓ cup shortening. By using rice and an egg white to make a new crust, all of that fat is eliminated!

Also, the cream and half of the cheese have been taken out of the same recipe and replaced with skim milk and tofu. The tofu replaces bulk and body lost by decreasing the cheese and omitting the heavy cream. Here, lowfat cheese is used for the cheese that remains in the recipe. As you can see from the nutritional information in the next column, the savings on calories, fat and cholesterol are substantial. The sodium stayed the same because of the salt used in cooking the rice; you can eliminate that to reduce the sodium.

To prepare our low-fat, low-cholesterol version of Mushroom and Leek Quiche, please turn to page 122.

Mushroom and Leek Quiche

~~Pastry for 9-inch One-Crust Pie~~ RICE CRUST
~~2 tablespoons margarine or butter~~ NONSTICK COOKING SPRAY
1 cup coarsely chopped fresh mushrooms (about 4 ounces)
1 cup thinly sliced leek (about 1 small)
~~½ 1~~ cup shredded LOW FAT ~~natural~~ Swiss cheese (~~4~~ 2 ounces)
~~3 eggs~~ 5 EGG WHITES
~~⅔ 1~~ cup ~~whipping (heavy) cream~~ ⅔ CUP MASHED SOFT TOFU / SKIM MILK
~~¼ ½~~ teaspoon salt
⅛ teaspoon ground nutmeg
4 drops red pepper sauce
2 DROPS YELLOW FOOD COLOR

Heat oven to 425°. Prepare pastry. Melt margarine in 10-inch skillet over medium heat. Cook mushrooms and leek in skillet 3 minutes, stirring occasionally, until tender. Place in pie plate. Sprinkle with cheese. Beat eggs slightly; beat in remaining ingredients. Pour over cheese. Bake 15 minutes. Reduce oven temperature to 325°. Bake 20 to 25 minutes or until knife inserted halfway between center and edge comes out clean. Let stand 10 minutes before cutting.

Nutrition for original version Mushroom and Leek Quiche:

6 servings

Per serving			
Calories	480	Fat	40 g
Protein	12 g	Unsaturated	22 g
Carbohydrate	19 g	Saturated	18 g
Sodium	420 mg	Cholesterol	180 mg

Nutrition for low-fat version Mushroom and Leek Quiche:

6 servings

Per serving:			
Calories	165	Fat	3 g
Protein	14 g	Unsaturated	2 g
Carbohydrate	19 g	Saturated	1 g
Sodium	420 mg	Cholesterol	10 mg

Chapter 2

Tasty Appetizers
and Snacks

♦ Use fruits and vegetables (steamed or uncooked) in place of chips and crackers.

♦ Make your own chips for saving on fat and calories. Toast thin bagel slices and pita bread wedges. Spicy Tortilla Chips (page 39) are a delicious option.

♦ Always read the labels on commercial cracker and snack products. When choosing purchases, look for items without animal fats (lard or tallow) or saturated fats.

♦ Avoid fried and otherwise fatty items. Potato chips and corn chips, of course, and deep-fat fried food, cheese curds, and mayonnaise- and cream cheese–based dips aren't diet-wise choices.

♦ Substitute lowfat or nonfat yogurt for sour cream or mayonnaise in your favorite recipes for dips and spreads. Cholesterol-free reduced-calorie mayonnaise or salad dressing is a step in the right direction, but substitute some lowfat or nonfat yogurt for part of it.

♦ Use Thick Yogurt (page 35) in place of cream cheese.

♦ Don't forget that herbs and spices give wonderful flavor to dips and spreads—without adding salt, as dry mixes can.

Bell Pepper Nachos (page 36), Chicken Satay (page 37)

Guacamole

Serve Spicy Tortilla Chips (page 39) with this favorite dip.

¾ cup lowfat cottage cheese
1 avocado, peeled and cut into fourths
¾ cup finely chopped seeded tomato (about 1 medium)
2 tablespoons chopped onion
2 tablespoons finely chopped cilantro
1 tablespoon lime juice
1 to 2 jalapeño chilies, seeded and finely chopped
1 tomatillo, finely chopped
1 clove garlic, finely chopped
Dash of pepper

Place cottage cheese and avocado in blender or food processor. Cover and blend or process on medium speed until smooth. Mix avocado mixture and remaining ingredients. Cover and refrigerate at least 1 hour. Stir before serving.

About 2⅓ cups dip

Per Tablespoon			
Calories	15	Fat	1 g
Protein	1 g	Unsaturated	1 g
Carbohydrate	1 g	Saturated	0 g
Sodium	20 mg	Cholesterol	0 mg

Green Herb Dip

¾ cup plain lowfat yogurt
¼ cup cholesterol-free reduced-calorie mayonnaise or salad dressing
¼ teaspoon salt
½ cup watercress leaves
½ cup fresh parsley leaves
¼ cup fresh basil
1 green onion (with top), cut into 1-inch pieces

Place yogurt, mayonnaise and salt in blender or food processor. Add remaining ingredients. Cover and blend or process about 30 seconds, stopping blender occasionally to scrape sides, until finely chopped. Cover and refrigerate about 1 hour or until slightly thickened and chilled. Serve with raw vegetables if desired.

About 1 cup dip

Per Tablespoon			
Calories	20	Fat	1 g
Protein	1 g	Unsaturated	1 g
Carbohydrate	1 g	Saturated	0 g
Sodium	75 mg	Cholesterol	0 mg

Green Herb Dip

Oriental Dip

Crisp, blanched pea pods, thickly sliced fresh mushrooms and carrots—sliced on the diagonal—are delicious dippers.

8 ounces soft tofu
½ cup lowfat cottage cheese
1 tablespoon low-sodium soy sauce
1 tablespoon chopped green onion (with top)
1 teaspoon grated gingerroot
1 tablespoon sesame seed, toasted

Place tofu, cottage cheese and soy sauce in blender or food processor. Cover and blend or process about 30 seconds or until smooth. Stir in onion and gingerroot. Cover and refrigerate at least 2 hours. Stir in sesame seed. Serve with raw vegetables or crackers if desired.

About 1½ cups dip

Per Tablespoon			
Calories	14	Fat	1 g
Protein	1 g	Unsaturated	1 g
Carbohydrate	1 g	Saturated	0 g
Sodium	45 mg	Cholesterol	0 mg

Black Bean Dip

Make your own low-fat chips easily from pita breads: Heat oven to 400°. Cut around outside edges of pita breads to separate layers. Cut each layer into 8 wedges. Place wedges on ungreased cookie sheet. Bake 8 to 10 minutes or until light brown and crisp.

1 tablespoon chopped green chilies
¼ cup chopped onion (about 1 small)
1 clove garlic, crushed
1 can (15 ounces) black beans, drained
½ cup plain nonfat yogurt
½ teaspoon ground cumin
¼ teaspoon salt

Place chilies, onion, garlic and beans in blender or food processor. Cover and blend or process until almost smooth. Stir in yogurt, cumin and salt. Serve cold, or heat in 1½-quart saucepan over medium heat, stirring frequently, until hot. Serve with chips or crackers.

MICROWAVE DIRECTIONS: Place dip in 1½-quart microwavable casserole. Microwave uncovered on high 3 to 4 minutes, stirring every minute, until hot.

About 2 cups dip

Per Tablespoon			
Calories	10	Fat	0 g
Protein	1 g	Unsaturated	0 g
Carbohydrate	2 g	Saturated	0 g
Sodium	55 mg	Cholesterol	0 mg

Caponata

This Italian appetizer is usually rather heavy with olive oil. Here is a lighter version, though, with all the traditional flavor. Serve with breadsticks or crackers.

½ cup chopped onion (about 1 medium)
2 cloves garlic, crushed
1 tablespoon olive oil
7 cups chopped, pared eggplant (about 1½ pounds)
¾ cup chopped tomato (about 1 medium)
2 tablespoons chopped fresh or 2 teaspoons dried basil
2 tablespoons red wine vinegar
¼ teaspoon salt
¼ teaspoon pepper

Cook onion and garlic in oil in 10-inch nonstick skillet over medium heat until onion is tender. Stir in eggplant and tomato. Cook uncovered 8 to 10 minutes, stirring frequently, until eggplant is very tender. Stir in remaining ingredients. Cover and refrigerate about 2 hours or until cool.

MICROWAVE DIRECTIONS: Place onion, garlic and oil in 3-quart microwavable casserole. Cover tightly and microwave on high 2 minutes 30 seconds to 3 minutes 30 seconds or until onion is tender. Stir in eggplant and tomato. Cover tightly and microwave 5 to 6 minutes, stirring after 3 minutes, until eggplant is very tender. Stir in remaining ingredients.

About 3 cups dip

Per Tablespoon			
Calories	10	Fat	0 g
Protein	0 g	Unsaturated	0 g
Carbohydrate	1 g	Saturated	0 g
Sodium	10 mg	Cholesterol	0 mg

Coeur à la Crème

The French coeur à la crème, a dessert only faintly sweetened and served with fruit, is traditionally made in heart-shaped molds of porcelain or straw; any mold with holes in the bottom will work nicely. Serve this savory version with vegetables and crackers.

2 cups plain nonfat yogurt
1 package (8 ounces) Neufchâtel cheese, softened
2 tablespoons chopped fresh or 2 teaspoons dried dill weed
2 tablespoons chopped fresh or 2 teaspoons dried chervil
2 tablespoons chopped fresh parsley
½ teaspoon salt
½ teaspoon pepper

Line 3-cup mold that has holes in bottom or 6-inch strainer with double-thickness cheesecloth or single paper coffee filter. Place mold in dish. Beat yogurt and cheese in medium bowl on medium speed until smooth. Stir in remaining ingredients. Mound mixture in mold. Cover mold and dish and refrigerate at least 24 hours. Unmold onto serving plate. Serve with cucumber slices and crackers if desired.

About 2¼ cups spread

Per Tablespoon			
Calories	20	Fat	2 g
Protein	1 g	Unsaturated	1 g
Carbohydrate	1 g	Saturated	<1 g
Sodium	65 mg	Cholesterol	5 mg

Following pages: Coeur à la Crème

Bell Pepper Spread

¾ cup finely chopped red bell pepper (about 1 medium)
¾ cup finely chopped yellow bell pepper (about 1 medium)
½ cup part-skim ricotta cheese
¼ cup chopped fresh parsley
2 tablespoons chopped fresh or 2 teaspoons dried basil
4 drops red pepper sauce
½ package (8-ounce size) Neufchâtel cheese

Mix all ingredients in medium bowl. Serve with Spicy Tortilla Chips (page 39) or crackers if desired.

About 2 cups spread

Per Tablespoon			
Calories	15	Fat	1 g
Protein	1 g	Unsaturated	0 g
Carbohydrate	1 g	Saturated	1 g
Sodium	20 mg	Cholesterol	5 mg

Chutney-glazed Yogurt Spread

Look for low-fat cholesterol-free crackers to accompany this spread. Use Thick Yogurt to make your own spreads. It is used in Chocolate Swirl Cheesecake with Raspberry Topping (page 194).

Thick Yogurt (below)
½ cup shredded lowfat Cheddar cheese (2 ounces)
1 tablespoon finely chopped green onion (with top)
½ teaspoon curry powder
1 jar (9 ounces) chutney (about 1 cup)
2 tablespoons chopped green onions (with tops)

Prepare Thick Yogurt. Mix yogurt, cheese, 1 tablespoon onion and the curry powder. Spread mixture about ¾ inch thick in shallow 8-inch serving dish. Top with chutney. Sprinkle with 2 tablespoons onions. Serve with plain toast rounds or crackers if desired.

About 2 cups spread

THICK YOGURT

Line 6-inch strainer with basket-style paper coffee filter or double-thickness cheesecloth. Place strainer over bowl. Spoon 4 cups plain nonfat yogurt into strainer. Cover strainer and bowl and refrigerate at least 12 hours, draining liquid from bowl occasionally.

Per Tablespoon			
Calories	35	Fat	0 g
Protein	2 g	Unsaturated	0 g
Carbohydrate	5 g	Saturated	0 g
Sodium	45 mg	Cholesterol	0 mg

Bell Pepper Spread (bottom), Chutney-glazed Yogurt Spread (top)

Southwestern Popcorn Snack

6 cups hot-air–popped popcorn
2 cups toasted oat cereal
2 tablespoons margarine
½ teaspoon chili powder
¼ teaspoon ground cumin
¼ teaspoon garlic powder
2 tablespoons grated Parmesan cheese

Mix popcorn and cereal in large bowl. Heat margarine, chili powder, cumin and garlic powder until margarine is melted. Drizzle over popcorn mixture; toss. Immediately sprinkle with cheese; toss. Store in tightly covered container.

MICROWAVE DIRECTIONS: Use 1 bag (3 ounces) light microwave popcorn, popped (measure 6 cups). Mix popcorn and cereal in large bowl. Place margarine, chili powder, cumin and garlic powder in microwavable bowl. Microwave uncovered on high 20 to 40 seconds or until margarine is melted. Continue as directed.

About 8 cups snack

Per Cup			
Calories	95	Fat	4 g
Protein	3 g	Unsaturated	3 g
Carbohydrate	12 g	Saturated	1 g
Sodium	130 mg	Cholesterol	1 mg

Bell Pepper Nachos

Ordinary nachos are made with tortilla chips. Bell peppers, used in their place, cut calories and fat. You will probably want to use a fork to eat this version of nachos.

½ green bell pepper, seeded and cut into 6 strips
½ red bell pepper, seeded and cut into 6 strips
½ yellow bell pepper, seeded and cut into 6 strips
½ cup salsa
2 tablespoons sliced ripe olives
3 tablespoons shredded part-skim mozzarella cheese

Cut bell pepper strips crosswise in half. Place on ungreased broilerproof pie plate, 9 × 1¼ inches. Top with salsa, olives and cheese.

Set oven control to broil. Broil with top 3 to 4 inches from heat about 3 minutes or until cheese is melted.

MICROWAVE DIRECTIONS: Place bell pepper pieces on microwavable plate. Top with salsa, olives and cheese. Cover with waxed paper and microwave on high 1 minute 30 seconds to 2 minutes, rotating plate ¼ turn after 1 minute, until cheese is melted.

6 servings (6 nachos each)

Per Serving			
Calories	40	Fat	2 g
Protein	2 g	Unsaturated	1 g
Carbohydrate	3 g	Saturated	1 g
Sodium	165 mg	Cholesterol	5 mg

Chicken Satay

An authentic, Asian satay consists of marinated meat or seafood grilled on skewers and served with a sauce. Hoisin and plum sauce replace the high-fat peanut sauce that usually accompanies satay.

1 pound boneless skinless chicken breasts
⅓ cup hoisin sauce
⅓ cup plum sauce
2 tablespoons sliced green onions (with tops)
1 tablespoon grated gingerroot
2 tablespoons dry sherry
2 tablespoons white vinegar

Trim fat from chicken breasts. Cut chicken lengthwise into ½-inch strips. Mix all ingredients except chicken in large glass or plastic bowl. Add chicken; toss to coat. Cover and refrigerate 2 hours.

Set oven control to broil. Remove chicken from marinade; drain. Reserve marinade. Thread 2 pieces chicken on each of twelve 10-inch skewers.* Place on rack in broiler pan. Broil with tops 3 to 4 inches from heat about 8 minutes, turning once, until done. Heat marinade to boiling in 1-quart saucepan. Serve with chicken.

12 appetizers

*If using bamboo skewers, soak skewers in water at least 30 minutes before using to prevent burning.

Per Appetizer			
Calories	80	Fat	2 g
Protein	8 g	Unsaturated	1 g
Carbohydrate	7 g	Saturated	<1 g
Sodium	85 mg	Cholesterol	25 mg

Curried Lamb Kabobs

1 pound lean lamb boneless shoulder
½ cup dry white wine
1 tablespoon Worcestershire sauce
1 tablespoon curry powder
1 large red bell pepper, cut into 24 pieces

Trim fat from lamb shoulder. Cut lamb into 1-inch cubes. Mix lamb, wine, Worcestershire sauce and curry powder in large bowl. Cover and refrigerate at least 4 hours but no longer than 24 hours.

Set oven control to broil. Remove lamb from marinade; reserve marinade. Thread lamb alternately with bell pepper on each of twelve 8-inch skewers.* Place on rack in broiler pan. Broil with tops 3 to 4 inches from heat 12 to 15 minutes, turning twice and brushing with marinade, until lamb is done.

*If using bamboo skewers, soak skewers in water at least 30 minutes before using to prevent burning.

12 appetizers

Per Appetizer			
Calories	70	Fat	3 g
Protein	7 g	Unsaturated	2 g
Carbohydrate	1 g	Saturated	1 g
Sodium	30 mg	Cholesterol	25 mg

Spicy Tortilla Chips

2 tablespoons margarine, melted
½ teaspoon chili powder
8 corn or flour tortillas (8 inches in diameter)

Heat oven to 400°. Mix margarine and chili powder; brush on one side of tortillas. Cut each into 12 wedges. Place on ungreased jelly roll pan, 15½ × 10½ × 1 inch. Bake uncovered 8 to 10 minutes or until crisp and golden brown; cool. (Tortillas will continue to crisp as they cool.)

96 chips

Per Chip:			
Calories	10	Fat	0 g
Protein	0 g	Unsaturated	0 g
Carbohydrate	1 g	Saturated	0 g
Sodium	3 mg	Cholesterol	0 mg

Tarragon Stuffed Eggs

½ cup Egg Substitute (page 116) or cholesterol-free egg product
¼ cup chopped watercress or fresh spinach
2 tablespoons cholesterol-free reduced-calorie mayonnaise or salad dressing
2 teaspoons chopped shallot
½ teaspoon chopped fresh or ¼ teaspoon dried tarragon
½ teaspoon white wine vinegar
⅛ teaspoon salt
Dash of pepper
4 hard-cooked eggs

Spray 8-inch nonstick skillet with nonstick cooking spray. Heat over medium-high heat. Pour Egg Substitute into skillet. As mixture begins to set at bottom and side, gently lift cooked portions with spatula so that thin, uncooked portion can flow to bottom. Avoid constant stirring. Cook 1 to 2 minutes or until thickened throughout but still moist; cool.

Mash cooked egg substitute with fork. Stir in remaining ingredients except hard-cooked eggs. Cut eggs lengthwise in half; discard yolks. Fill whites with egg substitute mixture, mounding lightly. Place on serving plate. Cover and refrigerate up to 24 hours. Garnish with thinly sliced ripe olives if desired.

4 servings (2 egg halves each)

Per Serving			
Calories	50	Fat	2 g
Protein	6 g	Unsaturated	2 g
Carbohydrate	2 g	Saturated	<1 g
Sodium	230 mg	Cholesterol	0 mg

Spicy Tortilla Chips, Salsa Verde (page 170)

Chinese Firecrackers

Twisted in a crisp phyllo wrapping, these sweet-and-sour appetizers look like little firecrackers.

1 teaspoon vegetable oil
½ pound ground turkey
1 cup finely chopped cabbage
½ cup shredded carrot (about 1 medium)
2 tablespoons finely chopped green onions (with tops)
1 tablespoon chili paste or puree
1 tablespoon dry white wine
1 teaspoon cornstarch
14 frozen phyllo leaves (13 × 9 inches), thawed
1 tablespoon plus 1 teaspoon vegetable oil
¾ cup sweet-and-sour sauce

Heat 1 teaspoon oil in 10-inch nonstick skillet. Cook ground turkey, cabbage, carrot and onions in oil over medium heat about 5 minutes, stirring frequently, until turkey is done and vegetables are crisp-tender. Stir in chili paste. Mix wine and cornstarch; stir into turkey mixture. Cook uncovered, stirring occasionally, until slightly thickened.

Heat oven to 375°. Cut phyllo leaves crosswise in half. Cover with damp towel to keep from drying out. Place 1 piece phyllo on flat surface. Brush with small amount of oil. Top with second piece phyllo. Place about 2 tablespoons turkey mixture on short end of phyllo; shape into about 4-inch log. Roll up phyllo and turkey mixture. Twist phyllo 1 inch from each end to form firecracker shape. Repeat with remaining phyllo and turkey mixture. Brush firecrackers with remaining oil.

Bake on ungreased cookie sheet 18 to 22 minutes or until phyllo is crisp and golden brown. Serve with sweet-and-sour sauce.

14 firecrackers

Per Firecracker			
Calories	190	Fat	3 g
Protein	7 g	Unsaturated	2 g
Carbohydrate	35 g	Saturated	<1 g
Sodium	210 mg	Cholesterol	10 mg

Stuffed Pattypan Squash

16 tiny pattypan squash (about 1½ inches in diameter)*
½ cup soft bread crumbs (about ¾ slice bread)
1 teaspoon chopped fresh or ¼ teaspoon dried thyme
¼ teaspoon salt
2 green onions (with tops), finely chopped
1 tablespoon grated Parmesan cheese

Heat oven to 350°. Heat 1 inch water to boiling. Add squash. Cook 6 to 8 minutes or until crisp-tender; drain. Cut off stem ends. Hollow out squash; reserve squash shells. Chop squash meat finely. Mix squash and remaining ingredients except cheese. Spoon 1 heaping teaspoon filling into each squash shell. Sprinkle with cheese. Place in ungreased square pan, 9 × 9 × 2 inches. Bake uncovered 10 to 12 minutes or until hot.

MICROWAVE DIRECTIONS: Place squash and 2 tablespoons water in square microwavable dish, 8 × 8 × 2 inches. Cover tightly and microwave on high 3 to 5 minutes or until crisp-tender; drain. Hollow out and fill squash shells as directed. Place in square dish. Cover tightly and microwave 2 to 3 minutes or until hot.

*8 small pattypan squash (about 2½ inches in diameter) can be substituted for the tiny squash. Spoon 1 heaping tablespoon filling into each squash shell.

8 servings (2 tiny squash each)

Per Serving			
Calories	15	Fat	0 g
Protein	1 g	Unsaturated	0 g
Carbohydrate	3 g	Saturated	0 g
Sodium	95 mg	Cholesterol	0 mg

Chinese Firecrackers, Stuffed Pattypan Squash

Chicken Terrine

Serve thinly sliced with crackers, or slice ½ inch thick and serve with Spinach-Herb Sauce (page 167).

¼ cup chopped fresh parsley
1½ pounds boneless skinless chicken breasts
2 tablespoons chopped shallots
1 tablespoon chopped fresh or 1 teaspoon dried thyme
1 tablespoon vegetable oil
1 teaspoon salt
2 egg whites
½ cup chopped red bell pepper (about 1 small)

Heat oven to 350°. Line loaf pan, 8½ × 4½ × 2½ inches, with aluminum foil. Sprinkle parsley in bottom of pan. Trim fat from chicken breasts. Cut chicken into 1-inch pieces. Place chicken in food processor. Cover and process until coarsely ground. Add remaining ingredients except bell pepper. Cover and process until smooth. Stir in bell pepper.

Spread in pan. Cover tightly with foil. Bake 1 hour; remove foil cover. Bake 20 to 30 minutes longer or until meat thermometer inserted in center registers 180°. Cover and let stand 1 hour. Refrigerate at least 3 hours. Invert onto serving platter. Remove pan and foil.

16 servings

Per Serving			
Calories	65	Fat	2 g
Protein	10 g	Unsaturated	2 g
Carbohydrate	1 g	Saturated	0 g
Sodium	175 mg	Cholesterol	30 mg

Vegetable Frittata

This frittata makes wonderful finger food. To serve as a first course, pass some Salsa Verde (page 170) or Cheese Sauce (page 166).

1 teaspoon vegetable oil
½ cup sliced zucchini
½ cup chopped red bell pepper (about 1 small)
¼ cup chopped onion (about 1 small)
1 package (9 ounces) frozen artichoke hearts, thawed and cut into fourths*
2 tablespoons chopped fresh parsley
¼ teaspoon salt
¼ teaspoon pepper
9 egg whites or 1½ cups cholesterol-free egg product**
4 drops yellow food color
2 tablespoons shredded Gruyère cheese

Heat oil in 10-inch nonstick skillet over medium-high heat. Sauté zucchini, bell pepper, onion and artichoke hearts in oil. Beat remaining ingredients except cheese; pour over vegetables.

Cover and cook over medium-low heat 8 to 10 minutes or until egg whites are set and bottom is light brown. Invert onto heatproof serving plate. Sprinkle with cheese. Let stand 5 minutes. Cut into 12 wedges.

*1 can (14 ounces) artichoke hearts, drained, can be substituted for the frozen artichoke hearts.

**If using cholesterol-free egg product, omit food color.

12 servings

Per Serving			
Calories	40	Fat	1 g
Protein	4 g	Unsaturated	0 g
Carbohydrate	3 g	Saturated	1 g
Sodium	105 mg	Cholesterol	2 mg

Chicken Terrine, Spinach-Herb Sauce (page 167)

Chapter 3

Meaty Main Dishes

- Rather than make floury sauces and gravies, just reduce pan juices to the desired consistency and concentration of flavor. Remove the fat from meat cooking juices; pour the juices into a fat separator (which has a spout coming from the bottom of the container—below the fat line, because fat rises to the liquid surface) or, refrigerate, then skim off congealed fat.

- Refrigerate, then skim, soups and stews.

- Select lean cuts of meat and trim off all visible fat before cooking.

- The higher the designated grade of meat, the more fat it contains. "Prime," the highest grade, is the most thoroughly marbled with fat. "Choice" is next, and the leanest is "Select."

- Avoid frying meats, a cooking method that only adds fat to a fatty situation. Use nonstick cookware so less added fat is needed in cooking.

- Meat roasted on a rack can't cook in (and reabsorb) its own fat.

- Baste meats with their own juices, broth, or water rather than margarine.

- Marinades don't have to be oil based. Use flavored vinegars, herbs and spices.

- Rib cuts of beef, pork, veal and lamb are fatty; loin cuts are leaner. Beef and veal flank and round cuts are relatively lean; leg and shoulder cuts should be examined for leanness before buying.

- When buying ground beef, choose extra-lean.

Herbed Pot Roast

Here is a traditional pot roast for the whole family, with enough for leftovers.

3-pound lean beef boneless rump roast
½ teaspoon cracked black pepper
2 cloves garlic, finely chopped
1 cup dry red wine or beef broth
1 cup water
½ cup beef broth
¼ cup chopped fresh parsley
1 tablespoon chopped fresh or 1 teaspoon dried thyme
5 whole cloves
3 bay leaves
10 new potatoes
5 medium carrots (about ¾ pound), cut in half
4 large parsnips (about 1 pound), pared and cut into eighths
2 medium onions, cut into eighths

Heat oven to 325°. Trim fat from beef roast. Mix pepper and garlic; rub on beef. Place in Dutch oven. Add wine, water, broth, parsley, thyme, cloves and bay leaves. Heat to boiling; reduce heat. Cover and simmer 2½ hours.

Turn beef over. Add remaining ingredients. (Add water if necessary.) Cover and simmer 45 to 60 minutes or until beef and vegetables are tender. Remove cloves and bay leaves. Serve beef and vegetables with pan juices.

10 servings

Per Serving			
Calories	325	Fat	9 g
Protein	29 g	Unsaturated	5 g
Carbohydrate	28 g	Saturated	4 g
Sodium	125 mg	Cholesterol	80 mg

Gingered Flank Steak

Fresh ginger and garlic add extraordinary fresh flavor. Try grilling the steak outdoors instead of broiling it.

1½-pound lean beef flank steak
⅓ cup lemon juice
2 tablespoons honey
1 tablespoon low-sodium soy sauce
2 teaspoons grated gingerroot or 1 teaspoon ground ginger
2 cloves garlic, crushed

Trim fat from beef steak. Cut both sides of beef into diamond pattern ⅛ inch deep. Place in shallow glass or plastic dish. Mix remaining ingredients; pour over beef. Cover and refrigerate at least 8 hours, turning occasionally.

Remove beef from marinade; reserve marinade. Spray broiler pan rack with nonstick cooking spray. Place beef on rack in broiler pan. Broil with top 3 inches from heat 12 to 14 minutes, turning once and brushing frequently with marinade, until desired doneness. Slice beef diagonally across grain into thin slices.

4 servings

Per Serving			
Calories	330	Fat	11 g
Protein	45 g	Unsaturated	6 g
Carbohydrate	11 g	Saturated	5 g
Sodium	230 mg	Cholesterol	135 mg

Gingered Flank Steak, Two-Potato Salad with Dill Dressing (page 159), Frosted Banana Bars (page 201)

Peppery Beef Tenderloin

Don't season this tenderloin with any extra salt before tasting; the salt in the canned broth seasons the meat perfectly.

¾ pound beef tenderloin
2 teaspoons chopped fresh or ½ teaspoon dried marjoram
2 teaspoons sugar
1 teaspoon coarsely ground pepper
1 tablespoon margarine
1 cup sliced fresh mushrooms (about 3 ounces)
1 small onion, thinly sliced
¾ cup beef broth
¼ cup dry red wine
1 tablespoon cornstarch

Trim fat from beef tenderloin. Cut beef into four ¾-inch slices. Mix marjoram, sugar and pepper; rub on both sides of beef slices. Cook beef in margarine in 10-inch nonstick skillet over medium heat 4 to 5 minutes on each side, turning once, until brown and medium doneness. Remove beef to platter; keep warm.

Cook mushrooms and onion in same skillet over medium heat about 2 minutes, stirring occasionally, until onion is crisp-tender. Mix broth, wine and cornstarch; pour into skillet. Cook over medium heat, stirring constantly, until mixture thickens and boils. Boil and stir 1 minute. Serve over beef and, if desired, with hot cooked rice or cholesterol-free noodles.

4 servings (with about ⅓ cup sauce each)

Per Serving			
Calories	210	Fat	10 g
Protein	20 g	Unsaturated	7 g
Carbohydrate	8 g	Saturated	3 g
Sodium	230 mg	Cholesterol	60 mg

Peppery Beef Tenderloin, Saucy Jerusalem Artichokes (page 154)

Southwest Fajitas

1-pound lean beef flank steak or skirt steak
¼ cup lime juice
2 teaspoons chili powder
1 teaspoon ground cumin
2 cloves garlic, crushed
4 flour tortillas (10 inches in diameter)
1 cup salsa
1 cup plain nonfat yogurt

Trim fat from beef steak. Prick beef with fork in several places. Mix lime juice, chili powder, cumin and garlic in shallow glass or plastic dish. Place beef in dish; turn to coat both sides. Cover and refrigerate at least 4 hours, turning beef occasionally.

Heat oven to 325°. Wrap tortillas in aluminum foil. Heat in oven about 15 minutes or until warm. Remove from oven; keep wrapped.

Set oven control to broil. Spray broiler pan rack with nonstick cooking spray. Place beef on rack in broiler pan. Broil with top 2 to 3 inches from heat 10 to 12 minutes, turning after 6 minutes, until medium doneness. Slice beef diagonally across grain into very thin slices.

Place ¼ of the beef slices, 2 tablespoons of the salsa and 2 tablespoons of the yogurt on center of each tortilla. Fold one end of tortilla up about 1 inch over beef mixture; fold right and left sides over folded end, overlapping. Fold down remaining end. Serve with additional salsa and yogurt if desired.

4 servings

Per Serving			
Calories	300	Fat	9 g
Protein	29 g	Unsaturated	7 g
Carbohydrate	26 g	Saturated	2 g
Sodium	415 mg	Cholesterol	70 mg

Beef Paillard

For a paillard, lean meat is pounded flat for quick cooking. Simple preparation and very little added fat make this a popular dish. Tip: Squeeze juice right from the lemon half onto the meat.

1-pound lean beef boneless sirloin steak
¼ teaspoon salt
¼ teaspoon cracked black pepper
2 teaspoons vegetable oil
1 tablespoon lemon juice
2 tablespoons chopped fresh parsley

Trim fat from beef steak. Cut beef into 4 pieces. Flatten each piece beef to ¼-inch thickness between waxed paper or plastic wrap. Sprinkle with salt and pepper.

Heat 1 teaspoon oil in 10-inch nonstick skillet over medium-high heat. Add 2 pieces beef. Cook 1 minute; turn. Sprinkle with half of the lemon juice. Cook about 1 minute longer or until desired doneness. Add remaining 1 teaspoon oil to skillet. Repeat with remaining 2 pieces beef and lemon juice. Sprinkle with parsley.

4 servings

Per Serving			
Calories	255	Fat	11 g
Protein	36 g	Unsaturated	7 g
Carbohydrate	0 g	Saturated	4 g
Sodium	230 mg	Cholesterol	105 mg

Oriental Beef with Rice Noodles

¾-pound lean beef boneless round steak
2 tablespoons sake (rice wine), sherry or chicken broth
1 tablespoon finely chopped gingerroot
2 teaspoons vegetable oil
½ teaspoon salt
1 clove garlic, crushed
4 ounces rice sticks
1 teaspoon vegetable oil
2 cups thinly sliced bok choy with leaves (about 3 large stalks)
½ cup sliced green onions (with tops)
1 can (15 ounces) straw mushrooms, drained*
2 tablespoons sake (rice wine), sherry or chicken broth

Trim fat from beef steak. Cut beef diagonally into ¼-inch strips. Mix beef, 2 tablespoons sake, the gingerroot, 2 teaspoons oil, the salt and garlic in medium glass or plastic bowl. Cover and refrigerate 30 minutes.

Place rice sticks in large bowl. Cover with hot water. Let stand 10 minutes; drain well. Chop coarsely.

Heat 1 teaspoon oil in wok. Add beef mixture; stir-fry about 5 minutes or until beef is done. Add rice sticks, bok choy, onions and mushrooms; stir-fry about 4 minutes or until bok choy is crisp-tender. Sprinkle mixture with 2 tablespoons sake.

*2 jars (4.5 ounces each) whole mushrooms, drained, can be substituted for the straw mushrooms.

4 servings (about 1¾ cups each)

Per Serving			
Calories	355	Fat	16 g
Protein	33 g	Unsaturated	13 g
Carbohydrate	22 g	Saturated	3 g
Sodium	700 mg	Cholesterol	80 mg

Beef in Mushroom Sauce

This is a rich-tasting, lower-fat variation on the theme of beef stroganoff.

¾ pound lean beef boneless round steak, about ½ inch thick
2½ cups sliced fresh mushrooms (about 8 ounces)
½ cup chopped onion (about 1 medium)
1 clove garlic, finely chopped
¼ cup dry red wine
2 tablespoons cornstarch
1 can (10½ ounces) condensed beef broth
⅛ teaspoon pepper
¾ cup plain nonfat yogurt
2 cups hot cooked rice or cholesterol-free noodles
2 tablespoons chopped fresh parsley

Trim fat from beef steak. Cut beef with grain into 2-inch strips. Cut strips diagonally across grain into ¼-inch slices. (For ease in cutting, partially freeze beef about 1½ hours.)

Spray 10-inch nonstick skillet with nonstick cooking spray. Heat over medium-high heat. Stir beef, mushrooms, onion and garlic into skillet. Cook uncovered about 4 minutes, stirring frequently, until beef is no longer pink. Stir in wine. Heat to boiling; reduce heat. Cover and simmer 10 minutes. Stir cornstarch into broth until dissolved. Stir into beef mixture. Cook over medium-high heat, stirring frequently, until thickened, about 2 minutes; remove from heat. Stir in pepper and yogurt. Heat to boiling; reduce heat. Cover and simmer 30 minutes, stirring occasionally, until beef is tender. Serve over rice. Sprinkle with parsley.

4 servings (about 1 cup beef mixture and ½ cup noodles each)

Per Serving			
Calories	370	Fat	6 g
Protein	32 g	Unsaturated	4 g
Carbohydrate	43 g	Saturated	2 g
Sodium	1,040 mg	Cholesterol	70 mg

Meat Loaf OK

¾ pound extra-lean ground beef
¾ pound ground turkey
½ cup regular oats
½ cup tomato puree
¼ cup chopped onion (about 1 small)
2 tablespoons chopped fresh parsley
½ teaspoon Italian seasoning
½ teaspoon salt
¼ teaspoon pepper
1 clove garlic, finely chopped

Heat oven to 350°. Mix all ingredients thoroughly. Press mixture evenly in ungreased loaf pan, 8½ × 4½ × 2½ or 9 × 5 × 3 inches, or shape into loaf in ungreased rectangular pan, 13 × 9 × 2 inches. Bake uncovered 1¼ to 1½ hours or until center is no longer pink.

MICROWAVE DIRECTIONS: Press mixture evenly in ungreased microwavable loaf dish, 9 × 5 × 3 inches. Cover with waxed paper and microwave on medium-high (70%) 18 to 22 minutes, rotating dish ½ turn after 9 minutes, until center is no longer pink. Remove from dish; place on serving platter. Cover and let stand 5 minutes.

8 servings

Per Serving			
Calories	145	Fat	6 g
Protein	18 g	Unsaturated	2 g
Carbohydrate	3 g	Saturated	4 g
Sodium	250 mg	Cholesterol	60 mg

Spicy Burgers

1 pound extra-lean ground beef
½ teaspoon chili powder
½ teaspoon pepper
¼ teaspoon salt
¼ teaspoon ground red pepper (cayenne)
1 clove garlic, finely chopped

Mix all ingredients thoroughly. Shape mixture into 4 patties, each ½ inch thick.

Heat 10-inch nonstick skillet until hot. Place patties in skillet; reduce heat to medium. Cover and cook 6 to 8 minutes, turning once, until desired doneness.

4 servings

Per Serving			
Calories	165	Fat	5 g
Protein	27 g	Unsaturated	2 g
Carbohydrate	1 g	Saturated	3 g
Sodium	205 mg	Cholesterol	75 mg

Beef-Barley Stew

This easy, hearty stew requires next to no kitchen preparation.

1 pound extra-lean ground beef
½ cup chopped onion (about 1 medium)
2 cups beef broth
⅔ cup uncooked barley
2 teaspoons chopped fresh or ½ teaspoon dried oregano
¼ teaspoon salt
¼ teaspoon pepper
1 can (16 ounces) whole tomatoes, undrained
1 can (8 ounces) sliced water chestnuts, undrained
1 package (10 ounces) frozen mixed vegetables

Heat oven to 350°. Spray 10-inch nonstick skillet with nonstick cooking spray. Cook ground beef and onion in skillet over medium heat, stirring occasionally, until beef is brown; drain. Mix beef mixture and remaining ingredients except frozen mixed vegetables in 3-quart casserole; break up tomatoes. Cover and bake 30 minutes. Stir in mixed vegetables. Cover and bake 30 to 40 minutes longer or until barley is done.

6 servings (about 1⅓ cups each)

Per Serving			
Calories	215	Fat	4 g
Protein	22 g	Unsaturated	2 g
Carbohydrate	21 g	Saturated	2 g
Sodium	545 mg	Cholesterol	50 mg

Beef-Barley Stew

Chili-stuffed Peppers

Half of the meat in these stuffed peppers has been replaced by beans. Try substituting beans for part of the meat in your favorite casseroles—it's better for you and more economical, too.

4 large red, yellow or green bell peppers
½ pound extra-lean ground beef
½ cup finely chopped onion (about 1 medium)
2 teaspoons chili powder
½ teaspoon ground cumin
1 can (16 ounces) kidney beans, drained
1 can (15 ounces) tomato puree
1 can (4 ounces) chopped green chilies, undrained

Heat oven to 350°. Cut bell peppers lengthwise in half. Remove seeds and membranes. Place peppers, cut sides up, in rectangular baking dish, 13 × 9 × 2 inches.

Cook ground beef and onion in 10-inch nonstick skillet over medium heat, stirring occasionally, until beef is brown; drain. Stir in remaining ingredients. Heat to boiling; reduce heat. Cover and simmer 10 minutes, stirring frequently.

Divide beef mixture evenly among peppers. Cover and bake 40 to 45 minutes or until peppers are tender.

MICROWAVE DIRECTIONS: Prepare peppers as directed above—except place in rectangular microwavable dish, 13 × 9 × 2 inches. Crumble ground beef into 3-quart microwavable casserole. Add onion. Cover loosely and microwave on high 2 to 4 minutes, stirring after 2 minutes, until beef is no longer pink; drain. Stir in remaining ingredients. Cover tightly and microwave 5 to 7 minutes, stirring after 3 minutes, until boiling. Divide beef mixture evenly among peppers. Cover tightly and microwave 10 to 12 minutes, rearranging peppers after 5 minutes, until peppers are tender. Let stand covered 5 minutes.

4 servings (2 pepper halves each)

Per Serving			
Calories	230	Fat	4 g
Protein	21 g	Unsaturated	1 g
Carbohydrate	31 g	Saturated	3 g
Sodium	740 mg	Cholesterol	40 mg

Dijon Veal Roast

This is a good way to cook shoulder and rump roasts, less tender cuts of meat. Mustard and rosemary flavor the delicious pan juices.

1½-pound lean veal shoulder or rump roast
1 tablespoon Dijon mustard
1 teaspoon chopped fresh or ¼ teaspoon dried rosemary
¼ teaspoon salt
1 cup sliced fresh mushrooms (about 3 ounces)
½ cup dry white wine or chicken broth
¼ cup chopped onion (about 1 small)

Heat oven to 325°. Trim fat from veal shoulder. Mix mustard, rosemary and salt. Coat veal with mustard mixture. Place veal in Dutch oven. Add remaining ingredients. Cover and bake about 1¼ hours, spooning pan juices over veal occasionally, until tender. Slice veal. Spoon mushrooms and onion over veal.

6 servings

Per Serving			
Calories	175	Fat	4 g
Protein	27 g	Unsaturated	3 g
Carbohydrate	2 g	Saturated	1 g
Sodium	165 mg	Cholesterol	75 mg

Chili-stuffed Peppers, Parmesan-Pepper Rolls (page 145)

Stuffed Veal Chops with Cider Sauce

4 lean veal loin chops, 1 inch thick (about
  6 ounces each)
1 cup soft bread crumbs (about 1½ slices bread)
½ cup chopped all-purpose apple
¼ cup chopped onion (about 1 small)
2 tablespoons chopped fresh parsley
2 tablespoons apple cider
¼ teaspoon salt
⅛ teaspoon ground allspice
Cider Sauce (below)

Trim fat from veal chops. Cut slit in each chop to form pocket. Mix remaining ingredients except Cider Sauce. Fill each pocket with about ⅓ cup mixture.

Spray 10-inch nonstick skillet with nonstick cooking spray. Heat skillet over medium-high heat. Cook veal in skillet about 7 minutes, turning once, until brown; reduce heat to low. Cover and cook 20 to 25 minutes or until done. Remove veal to serving platter; keep warm. Reserve ½ cup liquid in skillet (strain, if necessary). Prepare Cider Sauce. Serve with veal.

4 servings (with about ¼ cup sauce each)

CIDER SAUCE

1 cup apple cider
½ cup apple brandy
2 tablespoons white wine vinegar
1 teaspoon cornstarch
1 tablespoon water

Stir cider, brandy and vinegar into reserved veal liquid in skillet. Heat to boiling. Boil 6 to 8 minutes or until mixture is reduced to about 1 cup. Mix cornstarch and water; stir into cider mixture. Heat to boiling, stirring constantly. Boil and stir 1 minute.

Per Serving			
Calories	435	Fat	10 g
Protein	48 g	Unsaturated	9 g
Carbohydrate	17 g	Saturated	1 g
Sodium	390 mg	Cholesterol	135 mg

Veal with Asparagus

1 teaspoon vegetable oil
1 tablespoon finely chopped shallot
1 clove garlic, finely chopped
¾ pound thin slices lean veal round steak, or veal for
  scallopini
⅓ cup dry white wine
1 cup sliced fresh mushrooms (about 3 ounces)
2 teaspoons chopped fresh or ½ teaspoon dried thyme
*12 ounces asparagus spears, cut into 1-inch pieces**

Heat oil in 10-inch nonstick skillet over medium-high heat. Sauté shallot and garlic in oil; reduce heat to medium. Add veal. Cook about 3 minutes, turning once, until light brown. Stir in remaining ingredients. Heat to boiling; reduce heat. Cover and simmer about 12 minutes, stirring occasionally, until asparagus is crisp-tender.

4 servings (with about ½ cup vegetable mixture each)

*1 package (10 ounces) frozen asparagus cuts, thawed, can be substituted for the fresh asparagus.

MICROWAVE DIRECTIONS: Omit oil. Place veal in rectangular microwavable dish, 13 × 9 × 2 inches. Add remaining ingredients. Cover tightly and microwave on high 7 to 9 minutes, rearranging veal after 4 minutes, until asparagus is tender.

Per Serving			
Calories	150	Fat	7 g
Protein	14 g	Unsaturated	4 g
Carbohydrate	5 g	Saturated	3 g
Sodium	30 mg	Cholesterol	45 mg

Veal Stew Gremolata

Gremolata is an Italian garnish—or seasoning—made from parsley, lemon peel and garlic. Serve this dish with crusty bread.

1-pound lean veal shoulder
¾ cup finely chopped onion
¼ cup finely chopped carrot
¼ cup finely chopped celery
1 clove garlic, crushed
1 teaspoon vegetable oil
½ cup dry red wine or beef broth
1 tablespoon chopped fresh or 1 teaspoon dried basil
¼ teaspoon salt
1 can (15 ounces) tomato puree
1 large bell pepper, cut into wedges
8 ounces fresh mushrooms, cut in half
Gremolata (below)

Trim fat from veal shoulder. Cut veal into 1-inch pieces. Cook veal, onion, carrot, celery and garlic in oil in Dutch oven over medium-high heat 3 to 4 minutes, stirring occasionally, until veal is brown. Stir in remaining ingredients except Gremolata. Heat to boiling; reduce heat to low. Cover and cook 50 to 60 minutes, stirring occasionally, until veal is tender. Stir in Gremolata just before serving.

4 servings (about 1¼ cups each)

GREMOLATA

3 tablespoons finely chopped fresh parsley
1 tablespoon grated lemon peel
1 teaspoon finely chopped garlic

Mix all ingredients.

Per Serving			
Calories	265	Fat	6 g
Protein	31 g	Unsaturated	4 g
Carbohydrate	19 g	Saturated	2 g
Sodium	610 mg	Cholesterol	75 mg

Veal Goulash

2 medium onions, sliced
2 cloves garlic, crushed
1 tablespoon plus 1 teaspoon sweet Hungarian paprika
1 teaspoon caraway seed
2 teaspoons vegetable oil
1 pound lean veal stew meat, cut into 1-inch cubes
2 tablespoons tomato paste
1 can (15 ounces) tomato sauce
⅓ cup lowfat sour cream
2 cups hot cooked cholesterol-free noodles

Cook onions, garlic, paprika and caraway seed in oil in Dutch oven over medium heat about 6 minutes, stirring frequently, until onions begin to soften. Stir in veal, tomato paste and tomato sauce; reduce heat to low. Cover and simmer about 1 hour or until veal is tender. Stir in sour cream. Serve over noodles.

4 servings (about 1½ cups each)

Per Serving			
Calories	355	Fat	14 g
Protein	26 g	Unsaturated	9 g
Carbohydrate	32 g	Saturated	5 g
Sodium	680 mg	Cholesterol	80 mg

Following pages: Stuffed Veal Chops with Cider Sauce (page 56), Sour Cream Biscuits (page 142)

Veal with Spinach and Fettuccine

¾ pound thin slices lean veal round steak or veal for scallopini
1 cup sliced fresh mushrooms (about 3 ounces)
¼ cup chopped shallots
½ cup Madeira wine or beef broth
½ cup beef broth
2 teaspoons cornstarch
⅛ teaspoon pepper
1 package (10 ounces) frozen chopped spinach, thawed and well drained
2 cups hot cooked fettuccine

Cut veal crosswise into ¼-inch strips. Spray 10-inch nonstick skillet with nonstick cooking spray. Sauté veal, mushrooms and shallots in skillet over medium-high heat 3 to 5 minutes or until veal is done. Mix wine, broth, cornstarch and pepper. Stir wine mixture and spinach into skillet. Heat to boiling, stirring constantly. Boil and stir 1 minute. Serve over fettuccine.

4 servings (about ¾ cup meat mixture and ½ cup fettuccine each)

MICROWAVE DIRECTIONS: Decrease wine to ⅓ cup. Trim fat from veal. Cut veal crosswise into ¼-inch strips. Place veal, mushrooms and shallots in 2-quart micro-wavable casserole. Cover and microwave on high 5 to 6 minutes, stirring every 2 minutes, until veal is done; drain. Mix wine, broth, cornstarch and pepper. Stir wine mixture and spinach into casserole. Cover and microwave 4 to 5 minutes, stirring every 2 minutes, until thickened.

Per Serving			
Calories	255	Fat	7 g
Protein	20 g	Unsaturated	4 g
Carbohydrate	23 g	Saturated	3 g
Sodium	190 mg	Cholesterol	55 mg

Pork Chops with Peppers

4 lean pork loin chops, ½ inch thick
1½ teaspoons chopped fresh or ¼ teaspoon dried rosemary
1 teaspoon chopped fresh or ¼ teaspoon dried thyme
¼ teaspoon salt
1 clove garlic, crushed
¼ cup chopped onion (about 1 small)
1 small red bell pepper, cut into ¼-inch strips
1 small yellow bell pepper, cut into ¼-inch strips
¼ cup dry vermouth or low-sodium chicken broth

Spray 10-inch nonstick skillet with nonstick cooking spray. Trim fat from pork chops. Sprinkle pork with rosemary, thyme, salt and garlic. Cook pork in skillet over medium-high heat 6 to 7 minutes, turning once, until brown. Sprinkle with onion and bell peppers. Pour vermouth into skillet; reduce heat to low. Cover and simmer about 30 minutes or until pork is tender. Serve with pan juices.

4 servings

Per Serving			
Calories	200	Fat	11 g
Protein	20 g	Unsaturated	7 g
Carbohydrate	2 g	Saturated	4 g
Sodium	100 mg	Cholesterol	70 mg

Veal with Spinach and Fettuccine

Cranberry Pork Chops with Turnips

*4 lean pork loin chops, about ½ inch thick (about
    1 pound)*
2 teaspoons chopped fresh or ½ teaspoon dried sage
¼ teaspoon pepper
¼ cup chicken broth
*2 medium turnips (about ½ pound), pared and cut
    into 2 × ½ × ½-inch strips*
1 cup whole-berry cranberry sauce
½ cup chopped onion (about 1 medium)

Trim fat from pork chops. Cook pork in 10-inch nonstick skillet over medium heat until brown on both sides. Sprinkle with sage and pepper. Pour broth around pork. Layer turnips around pork. Cover and simmer 15 minutes. Mix cranberry sauce and onion; spoon onto pork. Cover and simmer about 15 minutes until turnips are tender and pork is done.

4 servings

Per Serving			
Calories	320	Fat	11 g
Protein	21 g	Unsaturated	7 g
Carbohydrate	33 g	Saturated	4 g
Sodium	160 mg	Cholesterol	70 mg

Caribbean Pork Tenderloin

The plantain, a less-sweet cousin of the banana, is a principal starch in the Caribbean. Tip: Partially freeze tenderloins to make it easier to slice them thinly.

2 lean pork tenderloins, about ½ pound each
1 teaspoon grated orange peel
½ cup orange juice
2 tablespoons lime juice
2 tablespoons chopped fresh cilantro
½ teaspoon cracked black pepper
2 cloves garlic, cut in half
1 teaspoon cornstarch
¼ teaspoon salt
1 teaspoon vegetable oil
1 large ripe plantain, cut into ¼-inch slices

Trim fat from pork tenderloin. Cut pork across grain into ⅛-inch slices. Mix orange peel, orange juice, lime juice, cilantro, pepper and garlic in large glass or plastic bowl. Stir in pork. Cover and refrigerate 30 minutes.

Remove pork from marinade and drain. Stir cornstarch and salt into marinade; reserve. Heat oil in 10-inch nonstick skillet over medium-high heat. Sauté pork in oil about 4 minutes or until no longer pink. Stir in plantain; sauté until brown. Stir in marinade mixture. Heat to boiling, stirring constantly. Boil and stir 1 minute.

4 servings (about 1 cup each)

Per Serving			
Calories	175	Fat	3 g
Protein	17 g	Unsaturated	2 g
Carbohydrate	20 g	Saturated	1 g
Sodium	175 mg	Cholesterol	50 mg

Cranberry Pork Chops with Turnips

Garlicky Pork with Basil

¾-pound lean pork tenderloin
1 teaspoon vegetable oil
¼ cup chopped fresh or 1 tablespoon plus 1 teaspoon
 dried basil
¼ cup chicken broth
⅛ teaspoon ground red pepper (cayenne)
4 cloves garlic, crushed

Trim fat from pork tenderloin. Cut pork crosswise into 8 pieces. Flatten each piece of pork to ¼-inch thickness between waxed paper or plastic wrap. Cook pork in oil in 10-inch nonstick skillet over medium-high heat about 3 minutes, turning once, until brown. Stir in remaining ingredients. Heat to boiling; reduce heat. Cover and simmer about 5 minutes or until pork is done.

4 servings

MICROWAVE DIRECTIONS: Omit oil. Prepare pork as directed. Place pork in rectangular microwavable dish, 13 × 9 × 2 inches. Mix remaining ingredients; pour over pork. Cover tightly and microwave on high 4 to 6 minutes, rearranging pork after 2 minutes, until pork is done.

Per Serving			
Calories	115	Fat	3 g
Protein	18 g	Unsaturated	2 g
Carbohydrate	2 g	Saturated	1 g
Sodium	90 mg	Cholesterol	55 mg

Zucchini-filled Pork Rolls

1½ cups shredded zucchini (about 1 medium)
1 clove garlic, crushed
2 tablespoons grated Parmesan cheese
¼ teaspoon pepper
4 lean boneless pork chops, about ¾ inch thick
 (about 1 pound)
1 teaspoon vegetable oil
½ cup dry white wine or chicken broth
1 tablespoon Dijon mustard

Squeeze zucchini with paper towels to remove moisture. Spray 10-inch nonstick skillet with nonstick cooking spray. Cook zucchini and garlic in skillet over medium heat about 3 minutes or until tender. Stir in cheese and pepper. Remove zucchini mixture from skillet; cool.

Trim fat from pork chops. Flatten each pork chop to ¼-inch thickness between waxed paper or plastic wrap. Spread one-fourth of the zucchini mixture over each piece of pork. Roll up; secure with wooden picks. Add oil and pork rolls to skillet. Cover and cook over medium heat 15 to 20 minutes, turning once, until done. Remove wooden picks. Remove pork rolls from skillet; keep warm.

Add wine to skillet. Cook over high heat 2 to 3 minutes or until reduced by half. Stir in mustard. Pour sauce over pork rolls.

4 servings (with about 1 tablespoon sauce each)

Per Serving			
Calories	305	Fat	22 g
Protein	19 g	Unsaturated	14 g
Carbohydrate	3 g	Saturated	8 g
Sodium	145 mg	Cholesterol	70 mg

Zucchini-filled Pork Rolls, Tangy Carrots with Grapes
(page 149)

Pork and Tofu Stir-fry

Tofu, the curd made from soybeans, has the most protein for its calories of all legume products. Without an assertive flavor of its own, it is a nice carrier for seasonings and sauces, and can be used alone or to extend meats.

½-pound lean pork boneless loin or leg
1 teaspoon cornstarch
1 teaspoon low-sodium soy sauce
1 cup Chinese pea pods (about 3½ ounces)
2 teaspoons vegetable oil
1 teaspoon finely chopped gingerroot or ½ teaspoon
*   ground ginger*
1 clove garlic, finely chopped
1 cup sliced fresh mushrooms (about 3 ounces)
¼ cup sliced green onions (with tops)
2 teaspoons oyster sauce
1 teaspoon low-sodium soy sauce
5 ounces firm tofu, cut into ½-inch cubes

Trim fat from pork loin. Cut pork into 2 × 1 × ⅛-inch slices. (For ease in cutting, partially freeze pork about 1½ hours.) Toss pork, cornstarch and 1 teaspoon soy sauce in medium glass or plastic bowl. Cover and refrigerate 20 minutes. Heat 1 inch water to boiling in 1½-quart saucepan. Add pea pods. Cover and boil 1 minute; drain. Immediately rinse with cold water; drain.

Heat oil in 10-inch nonstick skillet or wok over high heat. Add pork mixture, gingerroot and garlic; stir-fry about 3 minutes or until pork is no longer pink. Add mushrooms and onions; stir-fry 2 minutes longer. Add remaining ingredients; stir-fry until heated through and mixed thoroughly.

4 servings (about ½ cup each)

Per Serving			
Calories	165	Fat	9 g
Protein	15 g	Unsaturated	7 g
Carbohydrate	7 g	Saturated	2 g
Sodium	130 mg	Cholesterol	35 mg

Pork Ragout

1 pound lean boneless pork
1 teaspoon ground ginger
½ teaspoon ground coriander
¼ teaspoon ground allspice
1 can (10½ ounces) low-sodium chicken broth
1 cup pitted prunes, cut into fourths
½ cup dried apricot halves, cut in half
2 cups hot cooked rice

Heat oven to 350°. Trim fat from pork. Cut pork into 1-inch cubes. Place pork, ginger, coriander, allspice and broth in Dutch oven. Cover and bake 30 minutes. Stir in prunes and apricots. Cover and bake 30 to 45 minutes longer or until pork is tender. Stir before serving. Serve over rice.

4 servings (¾ cup ragout and ½ cup rice each)

Per Serving			
Calories	415	Fat	11 g
Protein	24 g	Unsaturated	7 g
Carbohydrate	56 g	Saturated	4 g
Sodium	450 mg	Cholesterol	80 mg

Spicy Black Bean and Pork Stew

4 cups water
½ cup dried black beans (about 4 ounces)
2 ancho chilies
¾ pound lean pork boneless shoulder
1½ cups chopped seeded peeled tomatoes (about 2 large)
½ cup chopped onion (about 1 medium)
½ cup dry red wine
1 tablespoon chopped fresh or 1 teaspoon dried sage
1 tablespoon chopped fresh or 1 teaspoon dried marjoram
½ teaspoon salt
½ teaspoon ground cumin
¼ teaspoon ground cinnamon
1 clove garlic, finely chopped
2 cups 1-inch cubes pared butternut squash
1 medium red bell pepper, cut into 1-inch pieces
2 tablespoons chopped cilantro

Heat water, beans and chilies to boiling in Dutch oven. Boil uncovered 2 minutes; remove from heat. Cover and let stand 1 hour. Remove chilies; reserve. Heat beans to boiling; reduce heat. Simmer covered for 1 hour.

Seed and coarsely chop chilies. Trim fat from pork shoulder. Cut pork into 1-inch cubes. Stir pork, chilies and remaining ingredients except squash, bell pepper and cilantro into beans. Heat to boiling; reduce heat. Cover and simmer 30 minutes, stirring occasionally. Stir in squash. Cover and simmer 30 minutes, stirring occasionally, until squash is tender. Stir in bell pepper and cilantro. Cover and simmer about 5 minutes or until bell pepper is crisp-tender.

4 servings (about 1⅓ cups each)

Spicy Black Bean and Pork Stew, Sour Cream Biscuits
(page 142)

Per Serving			
Calories	315	Fat	7 g
Protein	22 g	Unsaturated	5 g
Carbohydrate	34 g	Saturated	2 g
Sodium	330 mg	Cholesterol	50 mg

Scalloped Potatoes and Ham

A less-rich white sauce makes this good old favorite acceptable for low-fat diets. To prepare the potatoes ahead of time, slice and then soak in cold water to prevent discoloration; drain well before layering.

2 tablespoons margarine
3 tablespoons all-purpose flour
½ teaspoon dry mustard
¼ teaspoon salt
⅛ teaspoon pepper
2 cups skim milk
3 cups thinly sliced pared potatoes (about 3 medium)
1 cup diced fully cooked smoked extra-lean ham (about 6 ounces)
¼ cup finely chopped onion (about 1 small)

Heat oven to 350°. Spray 1½-quart casserole with nonstick cooking spray. Heat margarine in 1½-quart saucepan over medium heat until melted. Stir in flour, mustard, salt and pepper. Cook over medium heat, stirring constantly, until margarine is absorbed. Gradually stir in milk. Heat to boiling, stirring constantly. Boil and stir 1 minute.

Layer ⅓ of the potatoes, ½ of the ham, ½ of the onion and ⅓ of the sauce in casserole; repeat. Top with remaining potatoes and sauce. Cover and bake 30 minutes. Uncover and bake about 40 minutes longer or until potatoes are tender. Let stand 5 to 10 minutes before serving.

4 servings (about 1 cup each)

MICROWAVE DIRECTIONS: Decrease milk to 1¾ cups. Spray 2-quart microwavable casserole with nonstick cooking spray. Place margarine in 4-cup microwavable measure. Microwave uncovered on high 15 to 30 seconds or until melted. Stir in flour, mustard, salt and pepper until margarine is absorbed. Gradually stir in milk. Microwave uncovered 4 to 5 minutes, stirring every minute, until thickened. Layer potatoes, ham, onions and sauce in casserole as directed. Cover tightly and microwave on medium-high (70%) 16 to 20 minutes, stirring every 5 minutes, until potatoes are tender. Sprinkle with paprika if desired.

Per Serving			
Calories	305	Fat	9 g
Protein	18 g	Unsaturated	7 g
Carbohydrate	39 g	Saturated	2 g
Sodium	840 mg	Cholesterol	25 mg

Ham with Cabbage and Apples

4 cups shredded cabbage
½ cup chopped onion (about 1 medium)
1 tablespoon packed brown sugar
1 tablespoon cider vinegar
⅛ teaspoon pepper
1 large green cooking apple, pared, cored and cut into rings
4 extra-lean fully cooked ham steaks (about 3 ounces each)

Spray 10-inch nonstick skillet with nonstick cooking spray. Cook all ingredients except ham steaks in skillet over medium heat about 5 minutes, stirring frequently, until apple is crisp-tender. Place ham on cabbage mixture; reduce heat to low. Cover and cook about 10 minutes or until ham is hot.

4 servings (with about ¾ cup cabbage mixture each)

MICROWAVE DIRECTIONS: Mix all ingredients except ham steaks in rectangular microwavable dish, 12 × 7½ × 2 inches. Cover loosely and microwave on high 5 to 7 minutes, stirring after 2 minutes, until apple is crisp-tender. Place ham on cabbage mixture. Cover loosely and microwave 4 to 6 minutes, rotating dish ½ turn after 2 minutes, until ham is hot.

Per Serving			
Calories	200	Fat	5 g
Protein	23 g	Unsaturated	3 g
Carbohydrate	16 g	Saturated	2 g
Sodium	1,150 mg	Cholesterol	45 mg

Tarragon Lamb Chops

Pine nuts, known also as piñons and pignolis, add rich flavor and a little crunch to the sauce for these festive chops.

4 lean lamb shoulder chops, ¾ inch thick (about 1½ pounds)
¼ cup chopped onion (about 1 small)
2 tablespoons pine nuts
1 tablespoon chopped fresh or 1 teaspoon dried tarragon
¼ teaspoon salt
½ cup dry white wine or chicken broth

Trim fat from lamb chops. Cook lamb in 10-inch nonstick skillet over medium-high heat about 3 minutes on each side or until brown. Remove lamb from skillet. Sauté onion and pine nuts in same skillet. Return lamb to skillet. Sprinkle with tarragon and salt. Pour wine into skillet. Cover and cook about 20 minutes or until lamb is tender. Serve with wine sauce.

4 servings (with about 2 tablespoons sauce each)

Per Serving			
Calories	285	Fat	11 g
Protein	37 g	Unsaturated	7 g
Carbohydrate	2 g	Saturated	4 g
Sodium	230 mg	Cholesterol	130 mg

Lamb with Yogurt-Mint Sauce

⅔ cup plain nonfat yogurt
¼ cup firmly packed fresh mint leaves
2 tablespoons sugar
4 lamb loin chops, about 1 inch thick (about 1 pound)

Place yogurt, mint and sugar in blender or food processor. Cover and blend or process until smooth.

Set oven control to broil. Spray broiler pan rack with nonstick cooking spray. Trim fat from lamb chops. Place lamb on rack in broiler pan. Broil with tops 2 to 3 inches from heat 12 to 14 minutes, turning lamb after 6 minutes, until desired doneness. Serve with sauce.

4 servings (with about 3 tablespoons sauce each)

Per Serving			
Calories	255	Fat	9 g
Protein	34 g	Unsaturated	6 g
Carbohydrate	9 g	Saturated	3 g
Sodium	105 mg	Cholesterol	115 mg

Seasoned Lamb Patties

1 pound lean ground lamb
¼ cup dry bread crumbs
¼ cup chopped fresh or 2 tablespoons dried mint
1 teaspoon lemon pepper

Set oven control to broil. Mix all ingredients thoroughly. Shape mixture into 4 patties, each ½ inch thick. Spray broiler pan rack with nonstick cooking spray. Place patties on rack in broiler pan. Broil with tops about 3 inches from heat 8 to 10 minutes, turning once, until no longer pink inside. Serve with mint jelly if desired.

4 servings

MICROWAVE DIRECTIONS: Prepare patties as directed. Place in square microwavable dish, 8 × 8 × 2 inches. Cover with waxed paper and microwave on high 5 to 7 minutes, turning after 3 minutes, until no longer pink inside.

Per Serving			
Calories	180	Fat	9 g
Protein	23 g	Unsaturated	5 g
Carbohydrate	1 g	Saturated	4 g
Sodium	70 mg	Cholesterol	85 mg

Lamb with Yogurt-Mint Sauce

Chapter 4

Poultry and Fish Choices

- Chicken, turkey, Cornish hens and pheasant are less fatty than duck and goose. Turkey is a bit leaner than chicken, and white meat has somewhat less fat than dark meat.

- Remove skin and all visible fat before cooking. Most of poultry fat is in the skin, making it easier to remove than red meat fat, which tends to be marbled throughout.

- Skinned poultry can dry out easily, especially when baked or roasted, so a good covering can be essential in keeping the meat moist.

- Fin fish and shellfish are generally lower in fat than meats and poultry. Shellfish are higher than fin fish in cholesterol (shrimp are highest).

- Choose water-packed when buying canned tuna, salmon and sardines, to limit overall fat intake.

- Imitation crabmeat has less cholesterol—but more sodium—than real crabmeat. Balance sodium intake when enjoying this product.

- Avoid frying.

Chicken Breasts with Sun-dried-tomato Sauce (page 78)

Chicken and Artichokes

4 boneless skinless chicken breast halves (about
*   1 pound)*
1 can (14½ ounces) chicken broth
2 cups sliced fresh mushrooms (about 6 ounces)
¼ cup chopped onion (about 1 small)
1 teaspoon chopped fresh or ¼ teaspoon dried oregano
⅛ teaspoon pepper
1 cup frozen green peas
1 package (9 ounces) frozen artichoke hearts*
2 tablespoons cornstarch
2 tablespoons grated Parmesan cheese
2 cups hot cooked rice

Trim fat from chicken breast halves. Spray 10-inch nonstick skillet with nonstick cooking spray. Heat over medium heat. Cook chicken in skillet until brown on both sides. Reserve ½ cup broth. Stir remaining broth, the mushrooms, onion, oregano and pepper into skillet. Heat to boiling; reduce heat. Cover and simmer 8 minutes, stirring occasionally.

Stir in frozen peas and artichoke hearts. Heat to boiling. Cover and simmer 8 to 10 minutes, separating artichoke hearts after 5 minutes, until chicken is done and vegetables are tender. Remove chicken; keep warm. Mix reserved broth, the cornstarch and cheese. Stir into artichoke mixture. Heat to boiling, stirring constantly. Boil and stir 1 minute. Serve over chicken and rice.

4 servings (with about 1 cup sauce each)

MICROWAVE DIRECTIONS: Increase cornstarch to 3 tablespoons. Reserve ½ cup broth. Place chicken, remaining broth, the mushrooms, onion, oregano and pepper in 3-quart microwavable casserole. Cover and microwave on high 8 minutes. Stir in frozen peas and artichoke hearts. Cover and microwave 8 to 10 minutes, separating artichoke hearts and rotating casserole ½ turn after 4 minutes, until chicken is done and vegetables are tender. Remove chicken; keep warm. Mix reserved broth, the cornstarch and cheese. Stir into artichoke mixture. Microwave uncovered 3 to 5 minutes, stirring every minute, until mixture thickens and boils.

*1 can (14 ounces) artichoke hearts, drained, can be substituted for the frozen artichoke hearts.

Per Serving			
Calories	330	Fat	5 g
Protein	32 g	Unsaturated	2 g
Carbohydrate	37 g	Saturated	3 g
Sodium	880 mg	Cholesterol	80 mg

....

Oriental Barbecued Chicken

Chicken thighs can be substituted for the breasts here, but they have about 9 milligrams more cholesterol per serving.

4 boneless skinless chicken breast halves (about
*   1 pound)*
½ cup hoisin sauce
1 tablespoon sesame oil
1 tablespoon no-salt-added tomato paste
½ teaspoon ground ginger
2 cloves garlic, crushed

Set oven control to broil. Trim fat from chicken breast halves. Place chicken on rack in broiler pan. Mix remaining ingredients; brush on chicken. Broil with tops about 4 inches from heat 7 to 8 minutes or until brown; turn. Brush with sauce. Broil 4 to 5 minutes longer or until juices of chicken run clear. Heat remaining sauce to boiling. Serve with chicken.

4 servings

Per Serving			
Calories	305	Fat	9 g
Protein	49 g	Unsaturated	7 g
Carbohydrate	3 g	Saturated	2 g
Sodium	170 mg	Cholesterol	135 mg

Oriental Barbecued Chicken

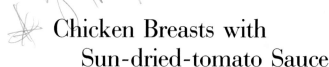

Chicken Breasts with Sun-dried-tomato Sauce

Use plain sun-dried tomatoes rather than those packed in oil.

¼ cup coarsely chopped sun-dried tomatoes
½ cup chicken broth
4 boneless skinless chicken breast halves (about 1 pound)
½ cup sliced fresh mushrooms (about 1½ ounces)
2 tablespoons chopped green onions (with tops)
2 cloves garlic, finely chopped
2 tablespoons dry red wine
1 teaspoon vegetable oil
½ cup skim milk
2 teaspoons cornstarch
2 teaspoons chopped fresh or ½ teaspoon dried basil
2 cups hot cooked fettuccine or rice

Mix tomatoes and broth; let stand 30 minutes.

Trim fat from chicken. Cook mushrooms, onions and garlic in wine in 10-inch nonstick skillet over medium heat about 3 minutes, stirring occasionally, until mushrooms are tender; remove mixture from skillet. Add oil to skillet. Cook chicken in oil over medium heat until brown on both sides. Add tomato mixture. Heat to boiling; reduce heat. Cover and simmer about 10 minutes, stirring occasionally, until chicken is done. Remove chicken; keep warm. Mix milk, cornstarch and basil; stir into tomato mixture. Heat to boiling, stirring constantly. Boil and stir 1 minute. Stir in mushroom mixture; heat through. Serve over chicken and fettuccine.

4 servings (with about ⅓ cup sauce each)

MICROWAVE DIRECTIONS: Decrease broth to ¼ cup. Omit oil. Decrease milk to ¼ cup. Mix tomatoes and broth as directed. Trim fat from chicken. Place mushrooms, onions, garlic and wine in 4-cup microwavable measure. Cover tightly and microwave on high 2 to 3 minutes or until mushrooms are tender; reserve. Place chicken in 2-quart microwavable casserole. Pour tomato mixture over chicken. Cover tightly and microwave on high 10 to 12 minutes, rotating casserole ¼ turn every 3 minutes, until chicken is done. Remove chicken; keep warm. Mix milk, cornstarch and basil; stir into tomato mixture. Microwave uncovered 2 to 4 minutes, stirring every minute, until mixture thickens and boils. Stir in mushroom mixture. Microwave uncovered 30 to 60 seconds or until mixture boils. Serve over chicken and fettuccine.

Per Serving			
Calories	345	Fat	4 g
Protein	46 g	Unsaturated	3 g
Carbohydrate	28 g	Saturated	1 g
Sodium	240 mg	Cholesterol	100 mg

Chicken Fajitas *good*

1 pound boneless skinless chicken breasts
2 tablespoons orange juice
2 teaspoons vegetable oil
1 teaspoon chili powder
¼ teaspoon salt
¼ teaspoon pepper
1 clove garlic, finely chopped
Chili Sour Cream (right)
4 flour tortillas (10 inches in diameter)
1 medium onion, sliced
1 medium green or red bell pepper, cut into
    ¼-inch strips
Chopped fresh cilantro

Trim fat from chicken breasts. Cut chicken with grain into ¼-inch slices. (For ease in cutting, partially freeze chicken about 1½ hours.) Mix orange juice, oil, chili powder, salt, pepper and garlic in medium glass or plastic bowl or heavy plastic bag. Add chicken; toss to coat. Cover and refrigerate at least 4 hours but no longer than 24 hours, turning chicken occasionally. Prepare Chili Sour Cream.

Heat oven to 350°. Wrap tortillas in aluminum foil. Bake 10 to 15 minutes or until warm. Remove from oven; keep tortillas wrapped. Remove chicken from marinade.

Heat 10-inch nonstick skillet or wok over high heat until 1 or 2 drops of water skitter when sprinkled in skillet. Add chicken; stir-fry 3 minutes. Add onion and bell pepper; stir-fry 3 to 4 minutes longer or until vegetables are crisp-tender.

For each serving, place ¼ of the chicken mixture and 2 tablespoons Chili Sour Cream in center of tortilla. Sprinkle with cilantro. Fold tortilla over filling.

4 servings

CHILI SOUR CREAM

½ cup lowfat sour cream
2 tablespoons orange juice
2 teaspoons chopped seeded jalapeño chili
¼ teaspoon ground cumin

Mix all ingredients. Refrigerate at least 1 hour.

Per Serving			
Calories	290	Fat	9 g
Protein	28 g	Unsaturated	7 g
Carbohydrate	22 g	Saturated	2 g
Sodium	240 mg	Cholesterol	90 mg

Curried Chicken and Nectarines

4 boneless skinless chicken breast halves (about 1 pound)
2 tablespoons reduced-calorie oil-and-vinegar dressing
1 teaspoon curry powder
¼ cup raisins
¼ cup sliced green onions (with tops)
¼ teaspoon salt
1 medium bell pepper, cut into ¼-inch strips
2 small nectarines, cut into ¼-inch slices

Trim fat from chicken breast halves. Cut chicken cross-wise into ½-inch strips. Mix dressing and curry powder in medium bowl. Add chicken; toss. Heat 10-inch nonstick skillet over medium-high heat. Stir in chicken and remaining ingredients except nectarines; stir-fry 4 to 6 minutes or until chicken is done. Stir in nectarines carefully; heat through. Serve with hot cooked rice or couscous if desired.

4 servings (about 1 cup each)

MICROWAVE DIRECTIONS: Prepare chicken as directed. Mix dressing and curry powder in 2-quart microwavable casserole. Add chicken; toss. Stir in remaining ingredients except nectarines. Cover tightly and microwave on high 8 to 10 minutes, stirring after 4 minutes, until chicken is done. Stir in nectarines carefully. Cover and microwave 1 minute or until heated through.

Per Serving			
Calories	210	Fat	6 g
Protein	25 g	Unsaturated	5 g
Carbohydrate	15 g	Saturated	1 g
Sodium	230 mg	Cholesterol	80 mg

Curried Chicken and Nectarines, Creamy Herb Dressing (page 160)

Spicy Cancun Drumsticks

Pour vegetable oil into a plastic spray bottle for homemade nonstick cooking spray. Lightly spritz the pan and chicken to keep the chicken from getting dry.

8 chicken drumsticks (about 1¾ pounds)
⅓ cup all-purpose flour
⅓ cup yellow cornmeal
1 teaspoon chopped fresh or ¼ teaspoon dried oregano
1 teaspoon chopped fresh or ¼ teaspoon dried basil
½ teaspoon ground cumin
½ teaspoon chili powder
¼ teaspoon salt
⅛ teaspoon ground cloves
⅓ cup buttermilk
¼ teaspoon red pepper sauce
Vegetable oil

Heat oven to 400°. Spray rectangular pan, 13 × 9 × 2 inches, with vegetable oil or nonstick cooking spray. Remove skin and fat from chicken drumsticks. Mix remaining ingredients except buttermilk, pepper sauce and oil in large plastic bag. Mix buttermilk and pepper sauce. Dip chicken in buttermilk mixture; shake in bag to coat with cornmeal mixture. Place in pan. Spray chicken lightly with oil or drizzle with 2 teaspoons oil. Bake uncovered 40 to 45 minutes or until juices run clear.

4 servings (2 drumsticks each)

MICROWAVE DIRECTIONS: Spray rectangular microwavable dish, 12 × 7½ × 2 inches, with vegetable oil or nonstick cooking spray. Prepare chicken as directed. Arrange chicken, thickest parts to outside edges, in dish. Cover loosely and microwave on high 8 to 12 minutes, rotating dish ½ turn after 5 minutes, until juices run clear.

Per Serving			
Calories	225	Fat	8 g
Protein	26 g	Unsaturated	6 g
Carbohydrate	11 g	Saturated	2 g
Sodium	120 mg	Cholesterol	80 mg

Tandoori Chicken with Raita

Raita, an Indian yogurt sauce, is a refreshing accompaniment to any spicy dish.

4 boneless skinless chicken breast halves (about 1 pound)
½ cup plain nonfat yogurt
1 tablespoon lemon juice
½ teaspoon salt
½ teaspoon paprika
¼ teaspoon ground cardamom
⅛ teaspoon ground ginger
⅛ teaspoon ground cumin
⅛ teaspoon crushed red pepper
1 clove garlic, finely chopped
    Raita (right)

Trim fat from chicken. Cut chicken with grain into ¼-inch strips. Mix remaining ingredients except Raita in medium glass or plastic bowl. Add chicken; toss to coat. Cover and refrigerate at least 4 hours but no longer than 24 hours, stirring occasionally.

Thread chicken strips on eight 11-inch skewers,* leaving space between each. Set oven control to broil. Place skewers on rack in broiler pan. Broil with tops 3 to 4 inches from heat 7 to 8 minutes, turning once, until done. Serve with Raita.

4 servings (with about ⅓ cup Raita each)

RAITA

1 cup plain nonfat yogurt
½ cup chopped seeded pared cucumber (about 1 small)
½ cup chopped seeded tomato (about 1 small)
2 tablespoons chopped cilantro
¼ teaspoon salt
¼ teaspoon ground cumin
⅛ teaspoon coarsely ground pepper

Mix all ingredients. Stir immediately before serving.

*If using bamboo skewers, soak skewers in water at least 30 minutes before using to prevent burning.

MICROWAVE DIRECTIONS: Prepare chicken as directed—except thread on eight 12-inch bamboo skewers. Arrange skewers in rectangular microwavable dish, 13 × 9 × 2 inches. Cover loosely and microwave on high 7 to 9 minutes, moving the 4 outside skewers to center after 4 minutes, until done.

Per Serving			
Calories	260	Fat	2 g
Protein	46 g	Unsaturated	1 g
Carbohydrate	10 g	Saturated	1 g
Sodium	600 mg	Cholesterol	100 mg

Chicken with Cilantro Pesto

Cilantro Pesto (below)
6 ounces uncooked fettuccine
2 teaspoons vegetable oil
1 cup 1-inch diagonal slices asparagus (about
*   4 ounces)*
1 cup sliced fresh mushrooms (about 3 ounces)
½ cup chopped onion (about 1 medium)
1½ cups cut-up cooked chicken or turkey (about
*   8 ounces)*

Prepare Cilantro Pesto. Cook fettuccine as directed on package; drain.

Heat oil in 10-inch nonstick skillet over high heat. Add asparagus, mushrooms and onion; stir-fry about 4 minutes or until asparagus is crisp-tender. Reduce heat. Stir in chicken and pesto thoroughly. Heat through; remove from heat. Add hot fettuccine to skillet; toss with 2 forks.

4 servings (about 1 cup each)

CILANTRO PESTO

¼ cup low-sodium chicken broth
1 tablespoon olive or vegetable oil
2 teaspoons lemon juice
¼ cup grated Parmesan cheese
1 tablespoon pine nuts
2 cloves garlic
1 cup firmly packed cilantro

Place all ingredients in blender or food processor in order listed. Cover and blend or process on medium speed, stopping occasionally to scrape sides, until almost smooth.

MICROWAVE DIRECTIONS: Prepare Cilantro Pesto and fettuccine as directed. Place oil, asparagus, mushrooms and onion in 3-quart microwavable casserole. Cover tightly and microwave on high 5 to 6 minutes, stirring after 3 minutes, until asparagus is crisp-tender. Stir in chicken and pesto. Cover tightly and microwave 2 to 3 minutes or until hot. Add hot fettuccine to casserole; toss with 2 forks.

Per Serving			
Calories	330	Fat	13 g
Protein	24 g	Unsaturated	10 g
Carbohydrate	30 g	Saturated	3 g
Sodium	150 mg	Cholesterol	55 mg

Chicken and Grape Pilaf

A traditional pilaf calls for cooking rice in hot fat before cooking it in hot broth. This version eliminates that step for a low-fat dish.

2 cups cubed cooked chicken or turkey
¾ cup uncooked regular long grain rice
¼ cup sliced green onions (with tops)
1¾ cups chicken broth
1 teaspoon margarine
¼ teaspoon ground cinnamon
¼ teaspoon ground allspice
⅛ teaspoon salt
1 cup seedless grape halves
2 tablespoons chopped pecans

Heat all ingredients except grape halves and pecans to boiling in 2-quart saucepan, stirring once or twice; reduce heat. Cover and simmer 14 minutes. (Do not lift cover or stir.) Remove from heat. Stir in grape halves and pecans, fluffing rice lightly with fork. Cover and let steam 5 to 10 minutes.

4 servings (about 1¼ cups each)

Per Serving			
Calories	210	Fat	9 g
Protein	23 g	Unsaturated	7 g
Carbohydrate	8 g	Saturated	2 g
Sodium	410 mg	Cholesterol	60 mg

Chicken-Basil Noodles

2 teaspoons olive or vegetable oil
½ cup finely chopped onion (about 1 medium)
1 clove garlic, finely chopped
2½ cups chopped tomatoes (about 3 medium)
2 cups cubed cooked chicken or turkey
¼ cup chopped fresh basil
½ teaspoon salt
⅛ teaspoon red pepper sauce
2 cups hot cooked cholesterol-free noodles

Heat oil in 10-inch nonstick skillet over medium-high heat. Sauté onion and garlic in oil. Stir in remaining ingredients except noodles; reduce heat to medium. Cover and cook about 5 minutes, stirring frequently, until mixture is hot and tomatoes are soft. Serve over noodles.

4 servings (about ¾ cup chicken mixture and ½ cup noodles each)

MICROWAVE DIRECTIONS: Omit olive or vegetable oil. Mix all ingredients except noodles in ungreased 2-quart microwavable casserole. Cover loosely and microwave on high 6 to 8 minutes, stirring every 2 minutes, until mixture is hot and tomatoes are soft. Serve over noodles.

Per Serving			
Calories	260	Fat	8 g
Protein	24 g	Unsaturated	6 g
Carbohydrate	23 g	Saturated	2 g
Sodium	340 mg	Cholesterol	60 mg

Orange Stir-fried Chicken

4 boneless skinless chicken breast halves (about 1 pound)
1 tablespoon low-sodium soy sauce
1 teaspoon cornstarch
1 teaspoon grated gingerroot or ½ teaspoon ground ginger
1 clove garlic, finely chopped
½ cup orange juice
2 teaspoons cornstarch
2 teaspoons vegetable oil
3 cups thinly sliced fresh mushrooms (about 8 ounces)
½ cup coarsely shredded carrot (about 1 medium)
2 cups hot cooked rice

Trim fat from chicken breast halves. Cut chicken into ¼-inch strips. Mix soy sauce, 1 teaspoon cornstarch, the gingerroot and garlic in medium glass or plastic bowl. Stir in chicken. Cover and refrigerate 30 minutes.

Mix orange juice and 2 teaspoons cornstarch until cornstarch is dissolved. Heat 1 teaspoon of the oil in 10-inch nonstick skillet over high heat. Add chicken mixture; stir-fry until chicken turns white. Remove chicken from skillet.

Add remaining 1 teaspoon oil to skillet. Add mushrooms and carrot; stir-fry about 3 minutes or until mushrooms are tender. Stir in chicken and orange juice mixture. Heat to boiling, stirring constantly. Boil and stir 30 seconds or until thickened. Serve over rice.

4 servings (about ¾ cup chicken mixture and ½ cup rice each)

Per Serving			
Calories	315	Fat	6 g
Protein	28 g	Unsaturated	5 g
Carbohydrate	35 g	Saturated	1 g
Sodium	630 mg	Cholesterol	80 mg

Orange Stir-fried Chicken

Sesame Chicken Salad

6 ounces uncooked bow-shaped pasta
Ginger Dressing (below)
1½ cups cut-up cooked chicken (about 8 ounces)
1 cup shredded bok choy leaves
1 cup very thinly sliced carrots (about 1½ medium)
¾ cup thinly sliced bok choy stems
1 tablespoon chopped seeded red chili
2 green onions (with tops), cut diagonally into ¼-inch slices

Cook pasta as directed on package; drain. Rinse with cold water; drain. Toss pasta and remaining ingredients. Cover and refrigerate at least 2 hours.

4 servings (about 2 cups each)

GINGER DRESSING

¼ cup lime juice
¼ cup honey
1 tablespoon vegetable oil
2 teaspoons sesame seed, toasted
2 teaspoons low-sodium soy sauce
1 teaspoon sesame oil
1 teaspoon finely chopped gingerroot or ½ teaspoon ground ginger

Mix all ingredients.

Per Serving			
Calories	355	Fat	9 g
Protein	20 g	Unsaturated	7 g
Carbohydrate	48 g	Saturated	2 g
Sodium	175 mg	Cholesterol	45 mg

Chicken-Vegetable Soup

This mildly flavored soup is chock full of vegetables. Don't add extra salt—it's in the broth.

4 cups chicken broth
2 cups cubed cooked chicken or turkey
1 cup small cauliflowerets*
1 cup cut-up fresh green beans*
1 teaspoon chopped fresh or ½ teaspoon dried tarragon
⅛ teaspoon pepper
4 small new potatoes, cut into fourths
1 medium carrot, sliced

Heat all ingredients to boiling; reduce heat. Cover and simmer 10 to 12 minutes, stirring occasionally, until vegetables are crisp-tender. Garnish each serving with tarragon sprig if desired.

4 servings (about 1½ cups each)

*1 cup frozen cauliflower and 1 cup frozen cut green beans can be substituted for the fresh cauliflowerets and green beans (do not thaw).

Per Serving			
Calories	300	Fat	7 g
Protein	28 g	Unsaturated	5 g
Carbohydrate	31 g	Saturated	2 g
Sodium	870 mg	Cholesterol	60 mg

From the menu, "At the Park" (page 21): Sesame Chicken Salad, Tarragon Stuffed Eggs (page 39), Basil-Red Pepper Muffins (page 144), Peppermint Brownies (page 199)

Creamy Chicken in Sage Popovers

Sage Popovers (right)
1 cup sliced fresh mushrooms (about 3 ounces)
⅔ cup sliced leek with top (about 1 small)
2 tablespoons chopped red bell pepper
2 tablespoons margarine
¼ cup all-purpose flour
1 teaspoon chopped fresh or ¼ teaspoon dried sage
⅛ teaspoon pepper
⅓ cup skim milk
1 can (10½ ounces) low-sodium chicken broth
1½ cups cut-up cooked chicken

Prepare Sage Popovers. While popovers are baking, cook mushrooms, leek and bell pepper in margarine in 2-quart nonstick saucepan over medium heat 5 minutes, stirring occasionally. Stir in flour, sage and pepper. Cook over low heat, stirring constantly, until liquid is absorbed; remove from heat. Gradually stir in milk and broth. Heat to boiling, stirring constantly. Boil and stir 1 minute. Stir in chicken; heat until hot. Serve in popovers.

4 servings (with about ½ cup chicken mixture each)

SAGE POPOVERS

⅓ cup all-purpose flour
⅓ cup skim milk
1 teaspoon chopped fresh or ½ teaspoon dried sage
2 teaspoons vegetable oil
Dash of salt
2 egg whites

Heat oven to 450°. Spray four 6-ounce custard cups generously with nonstick cooking spray. Beat all ingredients with hand beater until smooth. Fill custard cups about ½ full. Bake 20 minutes. Decrease oven temperature to 350°. Bake 15 to 20 minutes longer or until deep golden brown. Immediately remove from cups.

Per Serving			
Calories	255	Fat	13 g
Protein	23 g	Unsaturated	10 g
Carbohydrate	9 g	Saturated	3 g
Sodium	440 mg	Cholesterol	60 mg

Glazed Cornish Hens with Plums

Skinning game hens takes a little work, but it significantly reduces fat and cholesterol. Cut the skin along the backbone and peel back, working around to the front of the bird.

2 Rock Cornish hens, cut lengthwise in half and skinned
2 teaspoons vegetable oil
½ cup plum jam
¼ cup chopped onion (about 1 small)
1 tablespoon chopped fresh or 1 teaspoon dried sage
2 tablespoons lemon juice
2 tablespoons low-sodium soy sauce
2 cups cooked brown rice, hot
1¼ cups thinly sliced plums (about 2)

Heat oil in nonstick Dutch oven over medium-high heat. Cook hens in oil, turning once, until brown on both sides. Mix remaining ingredients except rice and plums; pour over hens. Heat to boiling; reduce heat. Cover and simmer 50 to 60 minutes or until juices run clear. Remove hens; reserve liquid in Dutch oven.

Spread rice on serving platter. Place hens on rice; keep warm. Add plums to reserved liquid. Heat to boiling; reduce heat to medium. Cook uncovered, stirring occasionally, until slightly thickened. Spoon sauce over hens and rice.

4 servings (with ½ cup rice and about 3 tablespoons sauce each)

Per Serving			
Calories	380	Fat	7 g
Protein	27 g	Unsaturated	5 g
Carbohydrate	52 g	Saturated	2 g
Sodium	620 mg	Cholesterol	90 mg

Turkey with Cranberry Stuffing

2 turkey breast tenderloins (about 1¼ pounds)
½ cup coarsely chopped cranberries
2 tablespoons packed brown sugar
1½ cups soft bread cubes
2 tablespoons sliced green onions (with tops)
2 tablespoons orange juice
½ teaspoon grated orange peel
¼ teaspoon salt
¼ teaspoon ground nutmeg
Nutmeg-Orange Sauce (below)

Heat oven to 400°. Spray square pan, 9 × 9 × 2 inches, with nonstick cooking spray. Cut pocket lengthwise in turkey breast tenderloins to within ½ inch of ends. Mix cranberries and brown sugar in medium bowl. Stir in remaining ingredients except Nutmeg-Orange Sauce. Spoon cranberry mixture into pockets in turkey; secure with wooden picks. Place in pan.

Cover and bake 40 to 45 minutes or until juices run clear. Serve with Nutmeg-Orange Sauce.

4 servings (with about 2 tablespoons sauce each)

NUTMEG-ORANGE SAUCE

1 tablespoon cornstarch
⅛ teaspoon ground nutmeg
Dash of salt
1 cup orange juice

Mix cornstarch, nutmeg and salt in 1½-quart saucepan. Gradually stir in orange juice. Cook over medium heat, stirring constantly, until mixture thickens and boils. Boil and stir 1 minute.

Per Serving			
Calories	270	Fat	3 g
Protein	35 g	Unsaturated	2 g
Carbohydrate	24 g	Saturated	1 g
Sodium	290 mg	Cholesterol	85 mg

Turkey Pot Pie

1 tablespoon margarine
¼ cup chopped onion (about 1 small)
1¼ cups chicken broth
2 tablespoons cornstarch
½ cup skim milk
1 teaspoon chopped fresh or ¼ teaspoon dried
  rosemary, crumbled
2 cups cut-up cooked turkey
1 package (10 ounces) frozen peas and carrots
Biscuit Crust (right)

Heat oven to 425°. Heat margarine in 2-quart sauce-pan over medium-high heat. Sauté onion in margarine; reduce heat to medium. Mix ¼ cup of the broth and the cornstarch. Stir cornstarch mixture, remaining broth, the milk and rosemary into onion mixture. Heat to boiling, stirring constantly. Boil and stir 1 minute. Stir in turkey and frozen peas and carrots; break up peas and carrots if necessary. Pour into ungreased square pan, 8 × 8 × 2 inches. Prepare Biscuit Crust; place on turkey mixture. Bake uncovered about 30 minutes or until bubbly and crust is golden brown.

4 servings

BISCUIT CRUST

1 cup all-purpose flour
1¼ teaspoons baking powder
⅛ teaspoon salt
1 tablespoon firm margarine
⅓ cup lowfat sour cream
3 tablespoons skim milk

Mix flour, baking powder and salt. Cut in margarine until mixture resembles fine crumbs. Mix sour cream and milk until smooth. Stir sour cream mixture into flour mixture until dough leaves side of bowl. Turn dough onto lightly floured surface. Roll gently in flour to coat. Knead lightly 10 times. Pat into 8-inch square. Cut into four 4-inch squares.

Per Serving			
Calories	385	Fat	11 g
Protein	30 g	Unsaturated	8 g
Carbohydrate	39 g	Saturated	3 g
Sodium	630 mg	Cholesterol	60 mg

Spicy Turkey-Tortilla Casserole

Oregano, cumin and red pepper perk up ground turkey in this layered casserole. For timid taste buds, you can omit the red pepper, since the Salsa Verde adds a little kick of its own.

1 pound ground turkey
½ cup chopped onion (about 1 medium)
¼ cup white wine vinegar
1 tablespoon chopped fresh or 1 teaspoon dried oregano
1 teaspoon paprika
½ teaspoon salt
½ teaspoon ground cumin
¼ teaspoon crushed red pepper
1 clove garlic, finely chopped
1 cup Salsa Verde (page 170) or green sauce
½ cup lowfat sour cream
½ cup chicken broth
8 corn tortillas (6 inches in diameter), cut into ½-inch strips
½ cup shredded lowfat Cheddar cheese (2 ounces)

Heat oven to 350°. Spray 10-inch nonstick skillet with nonstick cooking spray. Cook turkey, onion, vinegar, oregano, paprika, salt, cumin, red pepper and garlic in skillet over medium heat, stirring constantly, until turkey is brown.

Spread ½ cup of the Salsa Verde in bottom of ungreased square baking dish, 8 × 8 × 2 inches. Mix remaining salsa, the sour cream and broth. Layer half each of the tortilla strips, turkey mixture and sour cream mixture on salsa in dish; repeat. Sprinkle with cheese. Bake uncovered about 25 minutes or until hot and bubbly.

4 servings

MICROWAVE DIRECTIONS: Decrease chicken broth to ¼ cup. Crumble turkey into 2-quart microwavable casserole. Stir in onion, vinegar, oregano, paprika, salt, cumin, red pepper and garlic. Cover loosely and microwave on high 3 to 5 minutes, stirring every 2 minutes, until turkey is no longer pink. Spread ½ cup of the Salsa Verde in bottom of square microwavable dish, 8 × 8 × 2 inches. Mix remaining salsa, the sour cream and broth. Layer half each of the tortilla strips, turkey mixture and sour cream mixture on salsa in dish; repeat. Sprinkle with cheese. Cover loosely and microwave on high 6 to 8 minutes, rotating dish ¼ turn every 2 minutes, until center is hot. Let stand covered 5 minutes.

Per Serving			
Calories	435	Fat	20 g
Protein	33 g	Unsaturated	13 g
Carbohydrate	29 g	Saturated	7 g
Sodium	920 mg	Cholesterol	85 mg

Broiled Caribbean Swordfish

Papaya Salsa (below)
4 swordfish or shark steaks, 1 inch thick
  (about 1½ pounds)
¼ cup lime juice
¼ cup grapefruit juice
1 tablespoon grated lime peel
½ teaspoon salt
1 clove garlic, crushed

Prepare Papaya Salsa; cover and refrigerate. Place fish steaks in ungreased square dish, 8 × 8 × 2 inches. Mix remaining ingredients; pour over fish. Cover and refrigerate 2 hours.

Set oven control to broil. Spray broiler pan rack with nonstick cooking spray. Remove fish from marinade; reserve marinade. Place fish on rack in broiler pan. Broil with tops about 4 inches from heat about 16 minutes, turning and brushing with marinade after 8 minutes, until fish flakes easily with fork. Serve with salsa.

  4 servings (with about ½ cup salsa each)

PAPAYA SALSA

¼ cup finely chopped red bell pepper
2 to 3 tablespoons grapefruit juice
1 tablespoon finely chopped green onion (with top)
1 tablespoon chopped cilantro
⅛ teaspoon salt
1 large papaya, peeled, seeded and chopped (about
  2 cups)

Mix all ingredients. Cover and refrigerate.

MICROWAVE DIRECTIONS: Marinate fish steaks as directed. Remove fish from marinade. Arrange fish, thickest parts to outside edges, in rectangular microwavable dish, 12 × 7½ × 2 inches. Cover tightly and microwave on high 11 to 13 minutes, rotating dish ½ turn after 6 minutes, until fish flakes easily with fork. Let stand covered 3 minutes. Serve with salsa.

Per Serving			
Calories	240	Fat	6 g
Protein	35 g	Unsaturated	5 g
Carbohydrate	10 g	Saturated	1 g
Sodium	250 mg	Cholesterol	95 mg

Oven-poached Halibut

Serve with Lemony Cocktail Sauce (page 170) or Cucumber-Yogurt Sauce (page 170).

4 halibut steaks, 1 inch thick (about 1½ pounds)
¼ teaspoon salt
4 sprigs dill weed
4 slices lemon
5 black peppercorns
¼ cup dry white wine or water

Heat oven to 450°. Place fish steaks in ungreased rectangular baking dish, 12 × 7½ × 2 inches. Sprinkle with salt. Place dill weed sprig and lemon slice on each. Top with peppercorns. Pour wine over fish. Bake uncovered 20 to 25 minutes or until fish flakes easily.

  4 servings

MICROWAVE DIRECTIONS: Prepare as directed—except arrange fish steaks, thickest parts to outside edges, in rectangular microwavable dish, 12 × 7½ × 2 inches. Cover tightly and microwave on high 7 to 9 minutes, rotating dish ½ turn after 4 minutes, until fish flakes easily with fork. Let stand covered 3 minutes; drain.

Per Serving			
Calories	200	Fat	4 g
Protein	35 g	Unsaturated	3 g
Carbohydrate	1 g	Saturated	<1 g
Sodium	230 mg	Cholesterol	55 mg

Oven-poached Halibut

Italian Baked Bluefish

The blue-red flesh of bluefish lightens with cooking. For a less "fishy" flavor, remove the dark fatty stripe down the side of the fillet. Halibut or ocean perch can be substituted in this recipe with fine results.

1 pound bluefish or other medium-fat fish fillets
¼ cup dry red wine
2 tablespoons chopped ripe olives
1 tablespoon capers
4 anchovy fillets, drained and finely chopped
2 cloves garlic, crushed
1 can (28 ounces) Italian plum tomatoes, drained and chopped

Heat oven to 350°. Cut fish fillets into 4 serving pieces. Place in ungreased square baking dish, 8 × 8 × 2 inches. Mix remaining ingredients; pour over fish. Bake uncovered about 40 minutes or until fish flakes easily with fork.

4 servings

MICROWAVE DIRECTIONS: Decrease wine to 2 tablespoons. Cut fish fillets into 4 serving pieces. Arrange fish, thickest parts to outside edges, in square microwavable dish, 8 × 8 × 2 inches. Mix remaining ingredients; pour over fish. Cover loosely and microwave on high 9 to 11 minutes, rotating dish ¼ turn every 4 minutes, until fish flakes easily with fork.

Per Serving			
Calories	190	Fat	5 g
Protein	25 g	Unsaturated	4 g
Carbohydrate	7 g	Saturated	1 g
Sodium	310 mg	Cholesterol	65 mg

Tropical Mahimahi

1 pound mahimahi, flounder or other lean fish steaks, ¾ inch thick
⅓ cup orange juice
3 tablespoons lime juice
2 tablespoons honey
¼ teaspoon salt
1 clove garlic, crushed
1 cup Pineapple Salsa (page 173)

Cut fish steaks into 4 serving pieces. Place in ungreased square baking dish, 8 × 8 × 2 inches. Mix remaining ingredients except Pineapple Salsa; pour over fish. Cover and refrigerate at least 1 hour but no longer than 6 hours, turning once.

Set oven control to broil. Spray broiler pan rack with nonstick cooking spray. Remove fish from marinade; reserve marinade. Place fish on rack in broiler pan. Broil with tops about 4 inches from heat 12 to 15 minutes, turning and brushing with marinade after 6 minutes, until fish flakes easily with fork. Serve with Pineapple Salsa.

4 servings (with ¼ cup salsa each)

MICROWAVE DIRECTIONS: Prepare and marinate fish steaks as directed. Arrange fish, thickest parts to outside edges, in rectangular microwavable dish, 12 × 7½ × 2 inches. Cover tightly and microwave on high 8 to 10 minutes, rotating dish ½ turn after 4 minutes, until fish flakes easily with fork. Let stand covered 3 minutes. Serve with Pineapple Salsa.

Per Serving			
Calories	165	Fat	1 g
Protein	21 g	Unsaturated	1 g
Carbohydrate	17 g	Saturated	<1 g
Sodium	240 mg	Cholesterol	70 mg

Sole with Roasted Red Pepper Sauce

Both bell and jalapeño peppers can be roasted under the broiler or over a range-top flame. Due to the difference in size, it's not efficient to roast them together under the broiler. Brown the jalapeños over a burner while the bells broil, then toss them into the plastic bag together. Always use care when handling hot chilies; rubber gloves can be very helpful.

2 medium red bell peppers
1 jalapeño chili
⅓ cup lowfat sour cream
½ teaspoon sugar
1 pound sole or other lean fish fillets
4 cups bite-size pieces salad greens

Set oven control to broil. Place bell peppers on rack in broiler pan. Broil about 5 inches from heat 12 to 16 minutes, turning occasionally, until skin is blistered and evenly browned. Place peppers in plastic bag; close tightly. Let stand 15 to 20 minutes. Peel peppers; remove stem, seeds and membranes.

Hold jalapeño chili over range-top burner, using long-handled fork. Turn frequently until skin is blistered and evenly browned. Place chili in plastic bag; close tightly. Let stand 15 to 20 minutes. Peel chili; remove stem, seeds and membranes.

Place peppers and chili in blender or food processor. Cover and blend or process until smooth. Stir in sour cream and sugar.

Set oven control to broil. Cut fish fillets into 4 serving pieces. Place on rack in broiler pan. Broil with tops about 4 inches from heat 5 to 6 minutes or until fish flakes easily with fork (do not turn). Place salad greens on 4 serving plates. Top with fish. Serve with sauce.

4 servings (with about ¼ cup sauce each)

Per Serving			
Calories	180	Fat	7 g
Protein	23 g	Unsaturated	5 g
Carbohydrate	6 g	Saturated	2 g
Sodium	45 mg	Cholesterol	70 mg

Savory Fish en Papillote

1 pound orange roughy or other lean fish fillets
4 twelve-inch circles cooking parchment paper
4 teaspoons chopped fresh or 1 teaspoon dried oregano
¼ teaspoon salt
⅛ teaspoon pepper
1 small onion, thinly sliced
1 small tomato, thinly sliced
1 small zucchini, thinly sliced
¼ cup sliced ripe olives

Heat oven to 400°. Cut fish fillets into 4 serving pieces. Place each piece fish on half of each parchment circle. Sprinkle fish with oregano, salt and pepper. Layer onion, tomato, zucchini and olives on fish. Fold other half of circle over fish and vegetables. Beginning at one end, seal edge by turning up and folding tightly 2 or 3 times. Twist each end several times to secure. Place on ungreased cookie sheet.

Bake 20 to 25 minutes or until vegetables are crisp-tender and fish flakes easily with fork. To serve, cut a large X in top of each packet; fold back points.

4 servings

MICROWAVE DIRECTIONS: Prepare and wrap fish fillets and vegetables as directed. Arrange packets in circle in microwave oven. Microwave on high 7 to 8 minutes, rearranging packets after 4 minutes, until vegetables are crisp-tender and fish flakes easily with fork. Let stand 3 minutes before cutting X in packets.

Per Serving			
Calories	160	Fat	4 g
Protein	25 g	Unsaturated	3 g
Carbohydrate	5 g	Saturated	>1 g
Sodium	260 mg	Cholesterol	35 mg

Sea Bass and Leeks

West Coast sea bass and Florida black grouper are the same fish. The thickness of the fish will determine the cooking time, so checking for doneness is essential.

1½ cups sliced leeks with tops (about 2 medium)
1 pound sea bass or grouper fillets, skinned
¼ teaspoon salt
¼ teaspoon pepper
2 tablespoons chopped fresh parsley
½ cup dry white wine

Spread leeks evenly in 10-inch nonstick skillet. Cut fish fillets into 4 serving pieces. Place in single layer on leeks. Sprinkle with salt, pepper and parsley. Pour wine into skillet. Heat to boiling; reduce heat. Cover and simmer 12 to 15 minutes or until fish flakes easily.

4 servings

MICROWAVE DIRECTIONS: Decrease wine to ¼ cup. Spread leeks in square microwavable dish, 8 × 8 × 2 inches. Cut fish fillets into 4 serving pieces. Arrange fish on leeks with thickest parts to outside edges of dish. Sprinkle with salt, pepper and parsley. Pour wine into dish. Cover with waxed paper and microwave on high 8 to 11 minutes, rotating dish ½ turn after 4 minutes, until fish flakes easily with fork. Let stand covered 3 minutes.

Per Serving			
Calories	260	Fat	1 g
Protein	22 g	Unsaturated	<1 g
Carbohydrate	8 g	Saturated	<1 g
Sodium	340 mg	Cholesterol	70 mg

Savory Fish en Papillote, Zesty Fruit Salad (page 157)

Salmon with Dilled Cucumbers

4 salmon or halibut steaks, ¾ inch thick (about 1½ pounds)
1 tablespoon chopped fresh or ½ teaspoon dried dill weed
¼ teaspoon salt
¼ cup water
1 tablespoon lemon juice
Dilled Cucumbers (below)

Place fish steaks in 10-inch nonstick skillet. Sprinkle with dill weed and salt. Pour water and lemon juice into skillet. Heat to boiling; reduce heat. Cover and cook 15 to 20 minutes or until fish flakes easily. Meanwhile, prepare Dilled Cucumbers. Serve over fish.

4 servings (with about ¼ cup cucumbers each)

DILLED CUCUMBERS

1 medium pared cucumber
1 tablespoon chopped fresh or 1 teaspoon dried dill weed
1 tablespoon vinegar
1½ teaspoons sugar
¼ teaspoon salt

Cut cucumber lengthwise in half; seed and cut into thin slices. Mix cucumber and remaining ingredients in 1½-quart saucepan. Cook over high heat 1 to 2 minutes, stirring frequently, until cucumber is crisp-tender.

MICROWAVE DIRECTIONS: Arrange fish steaks, thickest parts to outside edges, in rectangular microwavable dish, 12 × 7½ × 2 inches. Sprinkle with dill weed and salt. Pour water and lemon juice over fish. Cover tightly and microwave on high 8 to 10 minutes, rotating dish ½ turn after 4 minutes, until fish flakes easily with fork. Let stand covered 3 minutes.

Prepare Dilled Cucumbers as directed—except place all ingredients in 1-quart microwavable casserole. Cover tightly and microwave on high 1 to 2 minutes or until cucumber is crisp-tender; drain. Serve over fish.

Per Serving			
Calories	205	Fat	4 g
Protein	36 g	Unsaturated	3 g
Carbohydrate	4 g	Saturated	<1 g
Sodium	370 mg	Cholesterol	55 mg

Fish and Fennel Rice

The anise flavor of fennel is a perfect complement to tarragon and spinach.

1 pound sole or other lean fish fillets
1 cup chopped fennel (about ½ bulb)
¼ cup chopped onion (about 1 small)
2 tablespoons water
2 cups chicken broth
1 cup uncooked regular long grain rice
1 cup shredded spinach (about 1½ ounces)
Paprika
1 tablespoon chopped fresh or 1 teaspoon dried tarragon
Lemon wedges

Cut fish fillets into 4 serving pieces. Cook fennel and onion in water in 10-inch nonstick skillet over medium heat about 4 minutes, stirring occasionally, until crisp-tender. Stir in broth, rice and spinach. Heat to boiling; reduce heat. Cover and simmer 10 minutes. Place fish on rice mixture. Cover and simmer 8 to 10 minutes longer or until fish flakes easily with fork and liquid is absorbed. Sprinkle fish with paprika and tarragon. Serve with lemon wedges.

4 servings (with about 1 cup rice each)

Per Serving			
Calories	350	Fat	7 g
Protein	27 g	Unsaturated	5 g
Carbohydrate	42 g	Saturated	2 g
Sodium	460 mg	Cholesterol	60 mg

Fish and Fennel Rice

Sole in Tomato Sauce

½ cup sliced fresh mushrooms (about 1½ ounces)
¼ cup dry white wine
1 tablespoon chopped fresh or ½ teaspoon dried thyme
1 tablespoon tomato paste
1½ cups chopped tomatoes (about 2 medium)
¼ cup chopped onion (about 1 small)
1 clove garlic, crushed
8 thin sole fillets (about 1 pound)
¼ teaspoon salt

Heat mushrooms, wine, half of the fresh thyme,* the tomato paste, tomatoes, onion and garlic to boiling in 10-inch nonstick skillet; reduce heat to medium. Cook uncovered about 10 minutes or until slightly thickened.

Sprinkle fish fillets with salt and remaining thyme. Roll up fish. Place on tomato mixture in skillet. Cover and cook over low heat about 15 minutes or until fish flakes easily with fork.

4 servings (with about ⅓ cup sauce each)

MICROWAVE DIRECTIONS: Reduce wine to 2 tablespoons. Mix mushrooms, wine, half of the fresh thyme,* the tomato paste, tomatoes, onion and garlic in rectangular microwavable dish, 10 × 6 × 1½ inches. Cover with waxed paper and microwave on high 4 to 6 minutes, stirring after 3 minutes, until onion is tender. Prepare and roll fish fillets as directed. Place on tomato mixture. Cover with waxed paper and microwave on high 8 to 10 minutes, rotating dish ½ turn after 4 minutes, until fish flakes easily with fork.

*Use full amount of dried thyme; omit sprinkling thyme on fish fillets.

Per Serving			
Calories	130	Fat	2 g
Protein	22 g	Unsaturated	1 g
Carbohydrate	5 g	Saturated	<1 g
Sodium	260 mg	Cholesterol	60 mg

Creamy Fish and Fruit Salad

The jalapeño dressing here is slightly spicy, so good with the juicy pieces of sweet fruit and orange roughy.

1 pound orange roughy or other lean fish fillets
3 cups bite-size pieces salad greens
1 medium cantaloupe or Persian melon (about 1½ pounds), pared and cut into thin wedges
2 cups bite-size pieces pineapple (about ½ medium)
1 pound seedless grapes, divided into small bunches
Creamy Jalapeño Dressing (below)
2 green onions (with tops), sliced

Set oven control to broil. Place fish fillets on rack in broiler pan. Broil with tops about 4 inches from heat 5 to 6 minutes or until fish flakes easily with fork (do not turn); cool. Flake fish. Place salad greens on serving platter or 4 salad plates. Arrange cantaloupe, pineapple, grapes and fish on greens. Top with Creamy Jalapeño Dressing. Sprinkle with onions.

4 servings

CREAMY JALAPEÑO DRESSING

¼ cup cholesterol-free reduced-calorie mayonnaise or salad dressing
¼ cup lowfat sour cream or plain nonfat yogurt
½ jalapeño chili, seeded and coarsely chopped

Place all ingredients in blender or food processor. Cover and blend or process until smooth.

MICROWAVE DIRECTIONS: Arrange fish fillets, thickest parts to outside edges, in rectangular microwavable dish, 12 × 7½ × 2 inches. Cover tightly and microwave on high 5 to 7 minutes, rotating dish ½ turn after 3 minutes, until fish flakes easily with fork; cool. Flake fish. Continue as directed.

Per Serving			
Calories	345	Fat	11 g
Protein	24 g	Unsaturated	8 g
Carbohydrate	39 g	Saturated	3 g
Sodium	180 mg	Cholesterol	70 mg

Hot Perch Salad

Use any combination of greens for this salad: Romaine, iceberg, Bibb, spinach or watercress.

2 tablespoons sliced almonds
1 tablespoon thinly sliced green onion (with top)
¼ teaspoon salt
⅛ teaspoon coarsely ground pepper
1 tablespoon margarine
½ cup orange juice
1 teaspoon cornstarch
1 pound ocean perch fillets
4 cups bite-size pieces salad greens
2 medium oranges, pared and sectioned

Cook almonds, onion, salt and pepper in margarine in 1½-quart saucepan about 4 minutes, stirring frequently, until almonds are light brown. Mix orange juice and cornstarch; stir into almond mixture. Cook about 30 seconds, stirring constantly, until thickened.

Set oven control to broil. Cut fish fillets into 4 serving pieces. Place on rack in broiler pan. Broil with tops about 4 inches from heat 5 to 6 minutes or until fish flakes easily with fork (do not turn). Arrange salad greens and orange sections on 4 salad plates. Top with fish. Spoon almond mixture over fish.

4 servings

MICROWAVE DIRECTIONS: Decrease orange juice to ⅓ cup. Mix almonds, onion, salt, pepper and margarine in 2-cup microwavable measure. Microwave uncovered on high 2 to 3 minutes, stirring every minute, until almonds are light brown. Mix orange juice and cornstarch; stir into almond mixture. Microwave uncovered on high 30 to 60 seconds or until thickened. Cut fish fillets into 4 serving pieces. Arrange fish, thickest parts to outside edges, in rectangular microwavable dish, 12 × 7½ × 2 inches. Cover tightly and microwave on high 5 to 7 minutes, rotating dish ½ turn after 3 minutes, until fish flakes easily with fork. Let stand covered 3 minutes. Continue as directed.

Per Serving			
Calories	210	Fat	7 g
Protein	23 g	Unsaturated	6 g
Carbohydrate	14 g	Saturated	1 g
Sodium	260 mg	Cholesterol	50 mg

Fish Burritos

Definitely not the traditional burrito, but something new and different.

4 flour tortillas (8 inches in diameter)
⅓ cup yellow cornmeal
½ teaspoon salt
1 pound scrod or other lean fish fillets, cut into 1-inch pieces
1 tablespoon vegetable oil
½ cup Salsa Verde (page 170) or green sauce

Heat oven to 300°. Wrap tortillas in aluminum foil. Heat in oven 15 minutes. Meanwhile, mix cornmeal and salt in small bowl. Coat fish with cornmeal mixture; shake off excess.

Heat oil in 10-inch nonstick skillet. Cook fish in oil over medium-high heat 6 to 7 minutes, turning occasionally, until fish flakes easily with fork. Divide fish among tortillas. Top each with 2 tablespoons Salsa Verde. Roll up tortillas.

4 servings

Per Serving			
Calories	225	Fat	7 g
Protein	25 g	Unsaturated	6 g
Carbohydrate	14 g	Saturated	1 g
Sodium	450 mg	Cholesterol	35 mg

Trout and Spinach Salad with Chutney Dressing

Chutney Dressing (below)
3 cups bite-size pieces spinach (about 6 ounces)
1 cup sliced fresh mushrooms (about 3 ounces)
½ cup bean sprouts
2 thin slices red onion, separated into rings
1 pound lake trout or other fatty fish fillets, skinned

Prepare Chutney Dressing. Toss spinach, mushrooms, bean sprouts, onion and half of the dressing. Place on 4 serving plates.

Set oven control to broil. Cut fish fillets into 4 serving pieces. Place on rack in broiler pan. Broil with tops about 4 inches from heat 5 to 6 minutes or until fish flakes easily with fork (do not turn). Place fish on spinach mixture. Pour remaining dressing over fish. Serve with freshly ground pepper if desired.

4 servings (with about 1¼ cups spinach mixture and 2 tablespoons dressing each)

CHUTNEY DRESSING

⅓ cup chutney, chopped if necessary
1 tablespoon vegetable oil
1 tablespoon lemon juice
⅛ teaspoon salt

Shake all ingredients in tightly covered container.

Per Serving			
Calories	240	Fat	8 g
Protein	26 g	Unsaturated	7 g
Carbohydrate	15 g	Saturated	1 g
Sodium	170 mg	Cholesterol	65 mg

Salmon Hash

Leftover potatoes are a terrific excuse to make this delicious hash.

1 tablespoon vegetable oil
½ cup chopped onion (about 1 medium)
½ cup chopped green bell pepper (about 1 small)
½ cup chopped red bell pepper (about 1 small)
¼ teaspoon salt
⅛ teaspoon pepper
1 clove garlic, crushed
2 cups diced cooked potatoes (about 2 medium)
1 can (16 ounces) salmon, drained and flaked
Lemon wedges

Heat oil in 10-inch nonstick skillet over medium-high heat. Sauté onion, bell peppers, salt, pepper and garlic in oil. Stir in potatoes and salmon. Cook uncovered, stirring frequently, until hot. Serve with lemon wedges.

4 servings (about 1 cup each)

Per Serving			
Calories	270	Fat	10 g
Protein	21 g	Unsaturated	7 g
Carbohydrate	23 g	Saturated	3 g
Sodium	460 mg	Cholesterol	40 mg

Trout and Spinach Salad with Chutney Dressing

Crab Pitas

1½ cups finely shredded cabbage
½ cup finely shredded red bell pepper
12 imitation crabmeat sticks (about 1 ounce each), chopped*
¼ cup sliced green onions (with tops)
¼ teaspoon red pepper sauce
¼ teaspoon salt
⅛ teaspoon pepper
4 pita breads (6 inches in diameter), cut in half and opened to form pockets
Yogurt Salsa (below)

Mix cabbage and bell pepper; set aside. Mix crabmeat, onions, pepper sauce, salt and pepper in 10-inch nonstick skillet. Cook over medium-high heat 3 to 5 minutes, stirring frequently, until hot. Fill pita breads with about ⅓ cup crabmeat mixture. Top with ½ cup cabbage mixture and 2 tablespoons Yogurt Salsa.

4 servings (2 half sandwiches each)

YOGURT SALSA

½ cup plain nonfat yogurt
½ cup chopped tomato (about 1 small)
2 tablespoons chopped green onions (with tops)
1 tablespoon chopped cilantro
¼ teaspoon ground cumin

Mix all ingredients.

*12 ounces shredded cooked crabmeat (about 2½ cups) can be substituted for the imitation crabmeat sticks.

Per Serving			
Calories	300	Fat	1 g
Protein	20 g	Unsaturated	1 g
Carbohydrate	58 g	Saturated	0 g
Sodium	950 mg	Cholesterol	15 mg

Fish and Spinach Chowder

1 cup water
¼ cup chopped onion (about 1 small)
1 medium potato, cut into ½-inch cubes
1 package (10 ounces) frozen chopped spinach
2 tablespoons margarine
3 tablespoons all-purpose flour
½ teaspoon salt
¼ teaspoon pepper
¼ teaspoon ground nutmeg
3 cups skim milk
1 tablespoon Worcestershire sauce
1 pound red snapper or other lean fish fillets, cut into 1-inch pieces

Heat water, onion, potato and frozen spinach to boiling in Dutch oven; reduce heat. Cover and simmer 5 minutes; break up spinach. Cover and simmer about 5 minutes longer or until potato is crisp-tender; drain. Reserve vegetables.

Heat margarine in Dutch oven over medium heat. Stir in flour, salt, pepper and nutmeg; remove from heat. Stir in milk and Worcestershire sauce. Heat to boiling over medium heat, stirring constantly. Boil and stir 1 minute. Stir in fish and vegetables. Heat to boiling; reduce heat. Cover and simmer about 10 minutes, stirring occasionally, until fish flakes easily with fork. Serve with freshly ground pepper and lemon wedges if desired.

4 servings (about 1½ cups each)

Per Serving			
Calories	350	Fat	12 g
Protein	31 g	Unsaturated	9 g
Carbohydrate	27 g	Saturated	3 g
Sodium	560 mg	Cholesterol	65 mg

Fish and Spinach Chowder

Marinated Shrimp Kabob Salad

1 tablespoon grated orange peel
½ cup orange juice
2 tablespoons vegetable oil
½ teaspoon salt
½ teaspoon crushed red pepper
2 cloves garlic, crushed
16 large raw shrimp, peeled and deveined
8 ounces jicama, pared and cut into 1-inch pieces
1 medium red bell pepper, cut into 1½-inch pieces
½ small pineapple, pared and cut into chunks
4 cups bite-size pieces salad greens

Mix orange peel, orange juice, oil, salt, red pepper and garlic in large glass or plastic bowl. Reserve ⅓ cup orange juice mixture; cover and refrigerate. Toss shrimp and remaining orange juice mixture in bowl. Cover and refrigerate at least 2 hours.

Set control to broil. Remove shrimp from marinade; reserve marinade. Alternate shrimp, jicama, bell pepper and pineapple on each of eight 10-inch skewers.* Place on rack in broiler pan. Broil with tops about 4 inches from heat about 8 minutes, turning and brushing once with marinade, until shrimp are pink. Place salad greens on 4 serving plates. Top each with 2 kabobs; remove skewers. Serve with reserved orange juice mixture.

4 servings

*If using bamboo skewers, soak skewers in water at least 30 minutes before using to prevent burning.

Per Serving			
Calories	185	Fat	8 g
Protein	11 g	Unsaturated	7 g
Carbohydrate	18 g	Saturated	1 g
Sodium	380 mg	Cholesterol	70 mg

Marinated Shrimp Kabob Salad

Scallops with Red Pepper Sauce

1 large red bell pepper, cut into fourths
⅛ teaspoon salt
10 drops red pepper sauce
1 clove garlic, finely chopped
¼ cup plain nonfat yogurt
¼ cup sliced green onions (with tops)
Cilantro leaves

Place steamer basket in ½ inch water in saucepan or skillet (water should not touch bottom of basket). Place bell pepper in basket. Cover tightly and heat to boiling; reduce heat. Steam 8 to 10 minutes or until tender.

Place bell pepper, salt, pepper sauce and garlic in blender or food processor. Cover and blend on medium speed until almost smooth. Heat in 1-quart saucepan over medium heat, stirring occasionally, until hot; remove from heat. Gradually stir in yogurt; keep warm.

Spray 10-inch nonstick skillet with nonstick cooking spray. Heat over medium-high heat. Add scallops and onions; stir-fry 4 to 5 minutes or until scallops are white in center. Serve sauce with scallops. Garnish with cilantro.

4 servings (with about 2 tablespoons sauce each)

MICROWAVE DIRECTIONS: Prepare bell pepper as directed—except place in 1-quart microwavable casserole. Add ¼ cup water. Cover tightly and microwave on high 4 to 5 minutes, stirring after 2 minutes, until tender; drain. Blend as directed. Pour into 1-quart microwavable casserole. Cover tightly and microwave on high 30 to 60 seconds or until hot. Stir in yogurt. Mix scallops and onions in 1½-quart microwavable casserole. Cover tightly and microwave on high 4 to 6 minutes, stirring every 2 minutes, until scallops are white in center; drain.

Per Serving			
Calories	115	Fat	1 g
Protein	20 g	Unsaturated	1 g
Carbohydrate	6 g	Saturated	0 g
Sodium	270 mg	Cholesterol	35 mg

Scallops with Red Pepper Sauce, Raspberry-Peppercorn Dressing (page 163)

Seafood Stew with Rosmarina

½ cup chopped green onions (with tops)
1 clove garlic, finely chopped
1 teaspoon vegetable oil
1 cup coarsely chopped tomato (about 1 large)
½ cup thinly sliced carrot (about 1 medium)
⅓ cup uncooked rosmarina (orzo) pasta
1 can (14½ ounces) chicken broth
1 bottle (8 ounces) clam juice
½ cup dry white wine
1 tablespoon chopped fresh or 1 teaspoon dried thyme
2 teaspoons chopped fresh or ½ teaspoon dried
*   dill weed*
¼ teaspoon salt
6 drops red pepper sauce
½ pound red snapper fillets, skinned and cut into
*   ½-inch pieces*
12 mussels, scrubbed and debearded
8 medium raw shrimp, peeled and deveined
½ cup sliced fresh mushrooms (about 1½ ounces)
Chopped fresh parsley
Lemon wedges

Cook onions and garlic in oil in nonstick Dutch oven over medium heat about 5 minutes, stirring occasionally. Stir in tomato, carrot, pasta, broth, clam juice, wine, thyme, dill weed, salt and pepper sauce. Heat to boiling; reduce heat. Cover and simmer about 20 minutes, stirring occasionally, until pasta is almost tender.

Stir in red snapper, mussels, shrimp and mushrooms. Cover and heat to boiling; reduce heat. Simmer 6 to 8 minutes, stirring occasionally, until fish flakes easily with fork and mussels open. Sprinkle with parsley. Serve with lemon wedges.

4 servings (about 1½ cups each)

Per Serving			
Calories	430	Fat	6 g
Protein	21 g	Unsaturated	5 g
Carbohydrate	57 g	Saturated	1 g
Sodium	900 mg	Cholesterol	50 mg

Seafood Stew with Rosmarina

Seafood-Ham Rolls

Low-sodium chicken broth is used here because lemon pepper contains salt, and because imitation crabmeat ("surimi," made from Pacific whitefish) has added sodium, too.

1 package (10 ounces) frozen asparagus spears
8 imitation crabmeat sticks (about 1 ounce each)
8 thin slices fully cooked smoked extra-lean ham (about 8 ounces)
¼ teaspoon lemon pepper
Lemon Sauce (right)

Heat oven to 400°. Rinse frozen asparagus spears under cold running water to separate; drain. Place 2 or 3 asparagus spears and 1 crabmeat stick on each slice ham. Sprinkle with lemon pepper. Roll ham around asparagus and crabmeat stick; secure with wooden picks. Place in ungreased rectangular baking dish, 12 × 7½ × 2 inches. Cover with aluminum foil and bake about 20 minutes or until asparagus is crisp-tender. Remove wooden picks. Serve ham rolls with Lemon Sauce.

4 servings

LEMON SAUCE

2 tablespoons cornstarch
2 teaspoons sugar
1 cup low-sodium chicken broth
1 tablespoon lemon juice

Mix cornstarch and sugar in 1½-quart saucepan. Gradually stir in broth. Cook over medium heat, stirring constantly, until mixture thickens and boils. Boil and stir 1 minute; remove from heat. Stir in lemon juice.

MICROWAVE DIRECTIONS: Prepare ham rolls as directed— except use microwavable rectangular dish. Cover with vented plastic wrap and microwave on high 6 to 8 minutes, rearranging ham rolls after 4 minutes, until asparagus is crisp-tender. Let stand covered while preparing Lemon Sauce. To prepare sauce, mix cornstarch and sugar in 4-cup microwavable measure. Gradually stir in broth. Microwave uncovered on high 3 to 4 minutes, stirring every minute, until mixture thickens and boils. Stir in lemon juice.

Per Serving			
Calories	195	Fat	4 g
Protein	24 g	Unsaturated	3 g
Carbohydrate	15 g	Saturated	1 g
Sodium	1,250 mg	Cholesterol	45 mg

Seafood Risotto

2 teaspoons vegetable oil
½ cup chopped onion (about 1 medium)
⅓ cup diced red bell pepper
1 clove garlic, finely chopped
¾ cup uncooked Arborio or short grain rice
¼ cup dry white wine
1 can (6½ ounces) minced clams, drained and liquid
   reserved
1 can (14½ ounces) chicken broth
½ cup water
1 package (6 ounces) frozen cooked shrimp, thawed
1 tablespoon chopped fresh parsley
2 tablespoons grated Parmesan cheese

Heat oil in 10-inch nonstick skillet over medium-high heat. Sauté onion, bell pepper and garlic in oil; reduce heat to medium. Stir in rice and wine. Cook and stir 30 seconds or until wine is absorbed.

Mix reserved clam liquid, the broth and water. Add ½ cup broth mixture to rice, stirring occasionally, until broth mixture is absorbed. Repeat with remaining broth mixture, adding clams, shrimp and parsley with last addition. Sprinkle with cheese.

4 servings (about ¾ cup each)

Per Serving			
Calories	305	Fat	5 g
Protein	20 g	Unsaturated	4 g
Carbohydrate	34 g	Saturated	1 g
Sodium	470 mg	Cholesterol	80 mg

Chapter 5

Meatless Mainstays

- ◆ Many egg dishes can be made without using the yolks, where cholesterol is concentrated. Try the Scrambled Egg Pockets on page 116.

- ◆ Some dishes traditionally made with several eggs can be successfully made with only 1 or 2 whole eggs plus several egg whites. Some delicious examples of this technique are Cheese-Garlic Soufflé, page 119, and Apple-Cheese Oven Pancake, page 122. One egg yolk contains about 217 mg cholesterol which, spread out among four servings, isn't bad at all.

- ◆ There are cholesterol-free egg substitutes available at supermarkets, both frozen and refrigerated. You can make your own substitute for whole eggs, too; see page 116.

- ◆ When cooking with cheese, use less than usual, and use a low-fat cheese.

- ◆ Legumes—canned and dried—are a low-fat, high-protein source of fiber (both soluble and insoluble).

- ◆ Lentils are especially convenient as they have a short cooking time compared to that of most dried beans and peas.

- ◆ Grains, pastas, nuts and seeds are good sources of complex carbohydrates. Combined with beans or peas, they can build nutritious meals with complete protein (a full complement of the necessary amino acids) but with no cholesterol, unless eggs or cheese are added.

Egg Substitute

For even color, combine egg and food color well before adding oil. One large egg equals about ¼ cup. Substitute the ½-cup recipe below for 2 whole eggs or ½ cup cholesterol-free egg product. Cover and refrigerate no longer than 2 days.

FOR ½ CUP

3 egg whites
3 drops yellow food color
1 teaspoon vegetable oil

FOR 1 CUP

6 egg whites
6 drops yellow food color
2 teaspoons vegetable oil

Mix egg whites and food color. Mix in oil. Cover and refrigerate up to 2 days.

2 or 4 servings (about ¼ cup each)

Per Serving			
Calories	45	Fat	2 g
Protein	5 g	Unsaturated	2 g
Carbohydrate	1 g	Saturated	0 g
Sodium	80 mg	Cholesterol	0 mg

Scrambled Egg Pockets

½ cup chopped seeded tomato (about 1 small)
¼ cup chopped onion (about 1 small)
2 tablespoons chopped green bell pepper
2 cups Egg Substitute (left) or cholesterol-free egg product
1 teaspoon chopped fresh or ½ teaspoon dried tarragon
¼ teaspoon salt
2 pita breads (6 inches in diameter), cut in half and opened to form pockets
½ cup alfalfa sprouts

Spray 10-inch nonstick skillet with nonstick cooking spray. Cook tomato, onion and bell pepper over medium heat about 3 minutes, stirring occasionally, until onion is tender. Mix Egg Substitute, tarragon and salt. Pour into skillet.

As mixture begins to set at bottom and side, gently lift cooked portions with spatula so that thin, uncooked portion can flow to bottom. Avoid constant stirring. Cook 3 to 5 minutes or until eggs are thickened throughout but still moist. Spoon into pita breads. Top with alfalfa sprouts.

4 servings

MICROWAVE DIRECTIONS: Place tomato, onion and bell pepper in 1½-quart microwavable casserole. Cover tightly and microwave on high 2 to 3 minutes, stirring after 1 minute, until onion is tender. Stir in Egg Substitute, tarragon and salt. Cover tightly and microwave 5 to 6 minutes, stirring every 2 minutes, until eggs are puffy and set but still moist.

Per Serving			
Calories	195	Fat	5 g
Protein	15 g	Unsaturated	4 g
Carbohydrate	23 g	Saturated	1 g
Sodium	450 mg	Cholesterol	0 mg

Brunch Eggs on English Muffins

Omit the Canadian-style bacon for a meatless dish.

Herbed Cheese Sauce (right)
2 English muffins, split
4 thin slices fully cooked Canadian-style bacon (about 2 ounces)
2 cups Egg Substitute (page 116) or cholesterol-free egg product

Prepare Herbed Cheese Sauce; keep warm. Toast English muffins. Cook bacon in 10-inch nonstick skillet over medium heat until brown on both sides.

Spray another 10-inch nonstick skillet with nonstick cooking spray. Heat over medium heat just until drop of water skitters when sprinkled in skillet. Pour Egg Substitute into skillet. As mixture begins to set at bottom and side, gently lift cooked portions with spatula so that thin, uncooked portion can flow to bottom. Avoid constant stirring. Cook 3 to 5 minutes or until thickened throughout but still moist.

Place 1 slice bacon on each muffin half. Top with eggs. Spoon about 2 tablespoons sauce over eggs.

4 servings (with about ½ cup scrambled egg and about 2 tablespoons sauce each)

HERBED CHEESE SAUCE

1 teaspoon margarine
2 teaspoons all-purpose flour
½ cup skim milk
¼ cup shredded lowfat Cheddar cheese (1 ounce)
2 teaspoons grated Parmesan cheese
½ teaspoon chopped fresh or ¼ teaspoon dried basil
Dash of ground red pepper (cayenne)

Heat margarine in 1-quart nonstick saucepan over low heat until melted. Stir in flour; remove from heat. Gradually stir in milk. Heat to boiling, stirring constantly. Boil and stir 1 minute; remove from heat. Stir in cheeses, basil and red pepper.

MICROWAVE DIRECTIONS: To make Herbed Cheese Sauce, place margarine in 2-cup microwavable measure. Microwave uncovered on high 15 to 20 seconds or until melted. Stir in flour. Stir in milk. Microwave uncovered 1 to 2 minutes, stirring every 30 seconds, until thickened. Stir in cheeses, basil and red pepper. Cover and let stand while preparing eggs and bacon. Spray 1½-quart microwavable casserole with nonstick cooking spray. Add Egg Substitute. Microwave uncovered on high 5 to 6 minutes, stirring with fork every 2 minutes until thickened throughout but still moist. Place bacon in single layer on 10-inch microwavable plate. Cover loosely and microwave on high 1 minute to 1 minute 30 seconds, rotating plate ½ turn after 30 seconds, until done.

Per Serving			
Calories	190	Fat	4 g
Protein	19 g	Unsaturated	3 g
Carbohydrate	19 g	Saturated	1 g
Sodium	670 mg	Cholesterol	5 mg

Eggs and Peppers

Colorful bell pepper strips make this a pretty dish.

1 teaspoon olive or vegetable oil
1 small onion, thinly sliced
½ red bell pepper, cut into ¼-inch strips
½ green bell pepper, cut into ¼-inch strips
½ yellow bell pepper, cut into ¼-inch strips
1 small tomato, cut into 1-inch pieces
2 cups Egg Substitute (page 116) or cholesterol-free egg product
½ teaspoon salt
⅛ teaspoon pepper

Heat oil in 10-inch nonstick skillet over medium-high heat. Sauté onion and bell peppers in oil. Stir in to-mato; heat through. Remove from skillet; keep warm.

Mix remaining ingredients; pour into skillet. Cook un-covered over medium heat. As mixture begins to set at bottom and side, gently lift cooked portions with spat-ula so that thin, uncooked portion can flow to bottom. Avoid constant stirring. Cook 3 to 5 minutes or until eggs are thickened throughout but still moist. Place eggs on platter. Mound vegetable mixture in center of eggs.

4 servings (about 1 cup each)

Calories	80	Fat	1 g
Protein	11 g	Unsaturated	1 g
Carbohydrate	7 g	Saturated	0 g
Sodium	435 mg	Cholesterol	0 mg

Tex-Mex Scrambled Eggs

2 teaspoons vegetable oil
3 corn tortillas (about 6 inches in diameter), cut into thin strips
¼ cup chopped onion (about 1 small)
2 cups Egg Substitute (page 116) or cholesterol-free product
½ jalapeño chili, seeded and chopped
1 cup salsa
¼ cup lowfat sour cream
2 tablespoons chopped green onions (with tops)

Heat oil in 10-inch nonstick skillet over medium-high heat. Cook tortillas and ¼ cup onion in oil about 5 minutes, stirring frequently, until tortillas are crisp.

Mix Egg Substitute and chili. Pour over tortilla mixture; reduce heat to medium. As mixture begins to set at bottom and side, gently lift cooked portions with spat-ula so that thin, uncooked portion can flow to bottom. Do not stir. Cook 4 to 5 minutes or until eggs are thickened throughout but still moist. Top each serving with salsa, sour cream and green onions.

4 servings (about 1 cup each)

Per Serving			
Calories	160	Fat	4 g
Protein	12 g	Unsaturated	3 g
Carbohydrate	18 g	Saturated	<1 g
Sodium	500 mg	Cholesterol	5 mg

Cheese-Garlic Soufflé

2 tablespoons margarine
3 cloves garlic, finely chopped
¼ cup all-purpose flour
¼ teaspoon dry mustard
⅛ teaspoon salt
Dash of ground red pepper (cayenne)
1 cup skim milk
1 cup shredded lowfat Cheddar cheese (4 ounces)
3 tablespoons grated Romano cheese
2 eggs, separated
2 egg whites
¼ teaspoon cream of tartar

Make a 4-inch band of triple-thickness aluminum foil 2 inches longer than circumference of 4-cup soufflé dish or 1-quart casserole. Secure foil band around dish. Spray inside of dish and foil with nonstick cooking spray.

Heat oven to 350°. Heat margarine in 2-quart saucepan over low heat. Cook garlic in margarine about 5 minutes, stirring occasionally, until garlic begins to turn golden. Stir in flour, mustard, salt and red pepper until margarine is absorbed; remove from heat. Gradually stir in milk. Heat over medium heat, stirring constantly, until mixture thickens and boils. Boil and stir 1 minute. Stir in cheeses until Cheddar cheese is melted; remove from heat.

Beat egg yolks in small bowl until thick and lemon colored. Gradually stir one-fourth of the hot cheese mixture into egg yolks; stir into remaining cheese mixture in saucepan. Beat 4 egg whites and cream of tarter in large bowl on high speed until stiff but not dry. Stir about one-fourth of the egg white mixture into cheese mixture. Fold cheese mixture into remaining egg white mixture.

Carefully pour into soufflé dish. Bake uncovered 50 to 60 minutes or until knife inserted halfway between center and edge comes out clean. Carefully remove foil band. Serve immediately.

4 servings

Per Serving			
Calories	240	Fat	14 g
Protein	16 g	Unsaturated	9 g
Carbohydrate	11 g	Saturated	5 g
Sodium	440 mg	Cholesterol	110 mg

Potato-Basil Scramble

2 cups cubed cooked potatoes (about 2 medium)
½ cup finely chopped onion (about 1 medium)
½ cup chopped red bell pepper (about 1 small)
2 cups Egg Substitute (page 116) or cholesterol-free egg product
2 tablespoons chopped fresh or 2 teaspoons dried basil
½ teaspoon salt
⅛ teaspoon ground red pepper (cayenne)

Spray 10-inch nonstick skillet with nonstick cooking spray. Cook potatoes, onion and bell pepper over medium heat about 5 minutes, stirring occasionally, until hot. Mix remaining ingredients; pour into skillet.

As mixture begins to set at bottom and side, gently lift cooked portions with spatula so that thin, uncooked portion can flow to bottom. Avoid constant stirring. Cook 3 to 5 minutes or until eggs are set and thickened throughout but still moist.

4 servings (about 1 cup each)

Per Serving			
Calories	190	Fat	5 g
Protein	13 g	Unsaturated	4 g
Carbohydrate	23 g	Saturated	1 g
Sodium	450 mg	Cholesterol	0 mg

Following pages: From the menu, "Bunch for Brunch" (page 21), clockwise from top left: Pumpkin-Fruit Bread (page 148), Mushroom and Leek Quiche (page 122), Citrus-Currant Scones (page 144), Potato-Basil Scramble

Mushroom and Leek Quiche

This rice crust is a fun, fat-free alternative to traditional pastry.

1½ cups hot cooked rice
1 egg white or 2 tablespoons cholesterol-free egg product
1 cup coarsely chopped fresh mushrooms (about 4 ounces)
1 cup thinly sliced leek (about 1 small)
½ cup shredded lowfat Swiss cheese (2 ounces)
⅔ cup mashed soft tofu
⅔ cup skim milk
¼ teaspoon salt
⅛ teaspoon ground nutmeg
5 egg whites or ¾ cup cholesterol-free egg product*
4 drops red pepper sauce
2 drops yellow food color

Heat oven to 350°. Spray quiche dish or pie plate, 9 × 1¼ inches, with nonstick cooking spray. Mix rice and 1 egg white. Spread evenly on bottom and side of pie plate, covering plate completely, using rubber spatula. Bake uncovered 5 minutes.

Increase oven temperature to 425°. Spray 10-inch nonstick skillet with nonstick cooking spray. Heat over medium heat. Cook mushrooms and leek in skillet 3 minutes, stirring occasionally, until tender. Place in pie plate. Sprinkle with cheese. Place remaining ingredients in blender or food processor. Cover and blend or process until smooth. Pour over cheese. Bake 15 minutes.

Reduce oven temperature to 325°. Bake 20 to 25 minutes or until knife inserted halfway between center and edge comes out clean. Let stand 10 minutes before cutting.

*If using cholesterol-free egg product, omit food color.

6 servings

Per serving			
Calories	165	Fat	3 g
Protein	14 g	Unsaturated	2 g
Carbohydrate	19 g	Saturated	1 g
Sodium	420 mg	Cholesterol	10 mg

Apple-Cheese Oven Pancake

Have the apple filling ready as soon as the pancake is done. You have to work quickly, or the pancake will deflate before you can fill it.

1 cup all-purpose flour
1 cup skim milk
¼ teaspoon salt
2 eggs
4 egg whites
1 tablespoon margarine
2 cups thinly sliced unpared tart cooking apples (about 2 medium)
2 tablespoons chopped fresh or 2 teaspoons dried chives
2 tablespoons sugar
¼ cup shredded lowfat Cheddar cheese (1 ounce)

Heat oven to 450°. Spray rectangular baking dish, 13 × 9 × 2 inches, with nonstick cooking spray. Beat flour, milk, salt, eggs and egg whites until smooth; pour into dish. Bake about 15 to 20 minutes or until puffy and golden brown.

Meanwhile, heat margarine in 10-inch nonstick skillet over medium-high heat. Sauté apples and chives in margarine. Stir in sugar. Spoon apple mixture onto pancake. Sprinkle with cheese. Bake about 1 minute or until cheese is melted.

4 servings

Per Serving			
Calories	295	Fat	7 g
Protein	14 g	Unsaturated	4 g
Carbohydrate	43 g	Saturated	3 g
Sodium	340 mg	Cholesterol	105 mg

Apple-Cheese Oven Pancake

Italian Frittata

It's easy to measure uncooked spaghetti, even if you don't have a kitchen scale. A 1-inch bundle of 10-inch-long spaghetti weighs about 3 ounces.

3 ounces uncooked spaghetti
1 tablespoon vegetable oil
3 tablespoons grated Parmesan cheese
1 cup sliced fresh mushrooms (about 3 ounces)
¼ cup chopped green onions (with tops)
2 teaspoons chopped fresh or ½ teaspoon dried oregano
¼ teaspoon salt
⅛ teaspoon pepper
1½ cups Egg Substitute (page 116) or cholesterol-free egg product
2 tablespoons shredded part-skim mozzarella cheese

Break spaghetti into about 2-inch pieces. Cook spaghetti as directed on package; drain. Toss spaghetti, oil and Parmesan cheese.

Spray 10-inch nonstick skillet with nonstick cooking spray. Cook mushrooms and onions over medium heat about 3 minutes, stirring occasionally, until mushrooms are tender; remove from heat.

Stir in spaghetti mixture, oregano, salt and pepper. Pour Egg Substitute into skillet. Cover and cook over medium-low heat 8 to 10 minutes or until eggs are set in center and light brown on bottom. Invert onto serving plate. Sprinkle with mozzarella cheese. Let stand 2 minutes.

4 servings

Per Serving			
Calories	155	Fat	5 g
Protein	12 g	Unsaturated	3 g
Carbohydrate	15 g	Saturated	2 g
Sodium	340 mg	Cholesterol	5 mg

Spinach Frittata with Creole Sauce

Spinach Frittata with Creole Sauce

Creole Sauce (below)
¼ cup chopped onion (about 1 small)
2 teaspoons margarine
3 cups coarsely chopped spinach (about 4 ounces)
1½ cups Egg Substitute (page 116) or cholesterol-free egg product
½ teaspoon chopped fresh or ⅛ teaspoon dried thyme
⅛ teaspoon salt
⅛ teaspoon pepper
2 tablespoons shredded part-skim mozzarella cheese

Prepare Creole Sauce; keep warm. Cook onion in margarine in 10-inch nonstick skillet over medium heat about 3 minutes, stirring occasionally. Add spinach; toss just until spinach is wilted.

Beat Egg Substitute, thyme, salt and pepper; pour over spinach. Cover and cook over medium-low heat 5 to 7 minutes or until eggs are set and light brown on bottom. Sprinkle with cheese. Cut into wedges. Serve with Creole Sauce.

4 servings

CREOLE SAUCE

1 cup coarsely chopped tomato (about 1 large)
¼ cup chopped onion (about 1 small)
2 tablespoons sliced celery
¼ teaspoon paprika
⅛ teaspoon pepper
4 drops red pepper sauce

Heat all ingredients to boiling in 1-quart saucepan, stirring occasionally; reduce heat. Simmer uncovered about 5 minutes, stirring occasionally, until thickened.

Per Serving			
Calories	95	Fat	3 g
Protein	11 g	Unsaturated	2 g
Carbohydrate	7 g	Saturated	1 g
Sodium	275 mg	Cholesterol	5 mg

Mexican Strata

Whole-grain bread gives this do-ahead dish a nice hearty texture, but white bread can be used too.

8 slices whole-grain bread (crusts removed)
1½ cups shredded lowfat Cheddar cheese (6 ounces)
1 can (4 ounces) chopped green chilies, well drained
1 jar (2 ounces) sliced pimientos, well drained
1⅓ cups skim milk
¼ teaspoon ground cumin
6 egg whites or 1 cup cholesterol-free egg product

Spray square baking dish, 8 × 8 × 2 inches, with nonstick cooking spray. Place 4 slices bread in dish. Sprinkle with cheese, chilies and pimientos. Top with remaining bread. Beat remaining ingredients; pour over bread. Cover and refrigerate at least 2 hours but no longer than 24 hours.

Heat oven to 325°. Bake 1 to 1¼ hours or until set and top is golden brown. Let stand 10 minutes before serving.

4 servings

Per Serving			
Calories	320	Fat	9 g
Protein	25 g	Unsaturated	3 g
Carbohydrate	32 g	Saturated	6 g
Sodium	830 mg	Cholesterol	5 mg

Easy Macaroni and Cheese

1 package (7 ounces) macaroni shells
Cheese Sauce (page 166)
2 tablespoons sliced green onions (with tops)
2 tablespoons chopped red bell pepper

Cook macaroni as directed on package; drain. Prepare Cheese Sauce in 3-quart saucepan. Stir macaroni, onions and bell pepper into sauce. Cook, stirring constantly, until heated through.

4 servings (about ¾ cup each)

Per Serving			
Calories	245	Fat	6 g
Protein	11 g	Unsaturated	3 g
Carbohydrate	35 g	Saturated	3 g
Sodium	170 mg	Cholesterol	1 mg

Three-Cheese Noodle Bake

This noodle dish is delicious with either Mushroom Sauce (page 167) or Salsa Verde (page 170).

4 ounces uncooked cholesterol-free noodles (about 2 cups)
1 cup lowfat cottage cheese
¾ cup shredded lowfat Cheddar cheese (3 ounces)
½ cup lowfat sour cream
⅓ cup chopped green onions (with tops)
3 tablespoons grated Parmesan cheese
½ teaspoon Worcestershire sauce
⅛ teaspoon pepper
1 egg
2 egg whites

Heat oven to 350°. Spray square baking dish, 8 × 8 × 2 inches, with nonstick cooking spray. Cook noodles as directed on package; drain. Mix noodles and remaining ingredients. Spread in dish. Bake uncovered 30 to 35 minutes or until center is set and edges are golden brown. Let stand 5 minutes.

4 servings

Per Serving			
Calories	370	Fat	8 g
Protein	25 g	Unsaturated	4 g
Carbohydrate	45 g	Saturated	4 g
Sodium	510 mg	Cholesterol	65 mg

Vegetable Manicotti

1 can (8 ounces) tomato sauce
8 uncooked manicotti shells
1 teaspoon olive or vegetable oil
½ cup shredded carrot (about 1 medium)
½ cup shredded zucchini
½ cup sliced fresh mushrooms (about 1½ ounces)
¼ cup sliced green onions (with tops)
1 clove garlic, finely chopped
¼ cup grated Parmesan cheese
2 tablespoons chopped fresh or 2 teaspoons dried basil
2 egg whites
1 container (15 ounces) part-skim ricotta cheese
½ cup shredded part-skim mozzarella cheese (2 ounces)

Heat oven to 350°. Spray rectangular baking dish, 12 × 7½ × 2 inches, with nonstick cooking spray. Pour ⅓ cup of the tomato sauce in dish. Cook manicotti shells as directed on package; drain.

Heat oil in 10-inch nonstick skillet over medium-high heat. Sauté carrot, zucchini, mushrooms, onions and garlic in oil. Stir in remaining ingredients except tomato sauce and mozzarella cheese. Fill manicotti shells with vegetable mixture; place in dish. Pour remaining tomato sauce over manicotti. Sprinkle with mozzarella cheese. Cover and bake 40 to 45 minutes or until hot and bubbly.

4 servings (2 manicotti shells each)

MICROWAVE DIRECTIONS: Spray rectangular microwavable dish, 12 × 7½ × 2 inches, with nonstick cooking spray. Pour ⅓ cup of the tomato sauce in dish. Cook manicotti shells as directed on package; drain. Omit olive oil. Place carrot, zucchini, mushrooms, onions and garlic in 1-quart microwavable casserole. Cover tightly and microwave on high 4 to 6 minutes or until tender; drain. Continue as directed. Cover tightly and microwave on high 8 to 10 minutes, rotating dish ½ turn after 4 minutes, until hot.

Per Serving			
Calories	250	Fat	13 g
Protein	20 g	Unsaturated	5 g
Carbohydrate	12 g	Saturated	8 g
Sodium	480 mg	Cholesterol	45 mg

Broccoli-Lasagne Roll-ups

4 uncooked lasagne noodles
1 jar (16 ounces) spaghetti sauce
1 cup part-skim ricotta cheese
1 cup shredded part-skim mozzarella cheese (4 ounces)
¼ cup grated Parmesan cheese
½ teaspoon salt
½ teaspoon ground nutmeg
⅛ teaspoon pepper
⅛ teaspoon red pepper sauce
1 package (10 ounces) frozen chopped broccoli, thawed
* and drained*

Heat oven to 350°. Cook noodles as directed on package; drain. Cover noodles with cold water. Pour 1 cup of the spaghetti sauce into ungreased square baking dish, 8 × 8 × 2 inches. Mix remaining ingredients. Drain noodles. Spread about ¾ cup of the cheese mixture to edges of each noodle. Roll up noodles. Place seam sides down on spaghetti sauce. Pour remaining spaghetti sauce over roll-ups. Cover and bake about 35 minutes or until sauce is hot and bubbly.

4 servings

MICROWAVE DIRECTIONS: Prepare as directed above—except use square microwavable dish, 8 × 8 × 2 inches. Cover tightly and microwave on high 10 to 12 minutes, rotating dish ½ turn every 4 minutes, until hot and bubbly.

Per Serving			
Calories	395	Fat	17 g
Protein	22 g	Unsaturated	9 g
Carbohydrate	39 g	Saturated	8 g
Sodium	1,160 mg	Cholesterol	55 mg

Three-Bean Chili

Garnish with chopped cilantro, lowfat sour cream or shredded lowfat Cheddar cheese if you like.

1 cup chopped onion (about 1 large)
2 cloves garlic, crushed
1 can (10½ ounces) low-sodium chicken broth
2 cups ½-inch pieces tomatoes (about 2 medium)
2 tablespoons chopped cilantro
1 tablespoon chopped fresh or 1 teaspoon dried oregano
2 teaspoons chili powder
1 teaspoon ground cumin
1 can (15 ounces) chili beans, undrained
1 can (8 ounces) kidney beans, undrained
1 can (8 ounces) garbanzo beans, undrained

Cook onion and garlic in ¼ cup of the broth in nonstick Dutch oven over medium heat about 5 minutes, stirring occasionally. Stir in remaining broth and remaining ingredients except beans. Heat to boiling; reduce heat. Cover and simmer 30 minutes, stirring occasionally.

Stir in beans. Heat to boiling; reduce heat. Simmer uncovered 20 minutes, stirring occasionally, until desired consistency.

4 servings (about 1¼ cups each)

MICROWAVE DIRECTIONS: Drain kidney and garbanzo beans. Mix onion and garlic in 3-quart microwavable casserole. Cover tightly and microwave on high 3 to 4 minutes, stirring after 2 minutes, until onion is crisp-tender. Stir in remaining ingredients. Cover tightly and microwave 12 to 15 minutes, stirring every 6 minutes, until boiling.

Per Serving			
Calories	250	Fat	2 g
Protein	13 g	Unsaturated	2 g
Carbohydrate	46 g	Saturated	0 g
Sodium	1,040 mg	Cholesterol	0 mg

Whole Wheat Ratatouille Calzone

Whole Wheat Calzone Dough (right)
2 teaspoons olive or vegetable oil
2 cups ½-inch cubes eggplant (about ½ pound)
1 cup sliced zucchini (about ⅔ medium)
½ cup coarsely chopped green bell pepper (about 1 small)
2 teaspoons chopped fresh or ½ teaspoon dried basil
1 teaspoon chopped fresh or ¼ teaspoon dried oregano
½ teaspoon salt
¼ teaspoon pepper
2 medium tomatoes, cut into eighths
1 small onion, thinly sliced
1 clove garlic, crushed
1 cup shredded part-skim mozzarella cheese (4 ounces)
2 tablespoons grated Parmesan cheese
1 egg white, beaten

Heat oven to 375°. Prepare Whole Wheat Calzone Dough.

Heat oil in 10-inch nonstick skillet over medium heat. Cook remaining ingredients except cheeses and egg white in oil uncovered, stirring frequently, until vegetables are tender and liquid is evaporated.

Spray cookie sheet with nonstick cooking spray. Divide Calzone Dough into 4 equal pieces. Pat each into 8-inch circle on lightly floured surface, turning dough over occasionally to coat lightly with flour. Top half of each circle with about ¾ cup vegetable mixture to within 1 inch of edge. Sprinkle cheeses over vegetable mixture. Fold dough over vegetable mixture; fold edge up and pinch securely to seal. Place on cookie sheet. Brush with egg white. Bake about 25 minutes or until golden brown.

4 calzones

WHOLE WHEAT CALZONE DOUGH

1 package active dry yeast
¾ cup warm water (105° to 115°)
1 tablespoon sugar
¾ teaspoon salt
1 tablespoon olive or vegetable oil
1¾ to 2¼ cups whole wheat flour

Dissolve yeast in warm water in large bowl. Stir in sugar, salt, oil and 1 cup of the flour. Beat until smooth. Mix in enough remaining flour to make dough easy to handle.

Turn dough onto lightly floured surface. Knead about 5 minutes or until smooth and elastic. Cover with bowl and let rest 5 minutes.

Per Calzone			
Calories	400	Fat	12 g
Protein	19 g	Unsaturated	6 g
Carbohydrate	58 g	Saturated	6 g
Sodium	890 mg	Cholesterol	20 mg

Whole Wheat Ratatouille Calzone, Marinated Fennel and Pepper Salad (page 158)

Spicy Rice with Black-eyed Peas

1 package (10 ounces) frozen black-eyed peas*
¾ cup uncooked instant rice
½ cup chopped onion (about 1 medium)
¼ cup chopped red bell pepper
1 tablespoon chopped fresh or 1 teaspoon dried oregano
¼ teaspoon salt
⅛ teaspoon ground red pepper (cayenne)
1 clove garlic, finely chopped
1 can (16 ounces) whole tomatoes, undrained

Cook peas as directed on package, using 10-inch nonstick skillet; drain. Stir in remaining ingredients; break up tomatoes. Heat to boiling; reduce heat. Cover and simmer about 10 minutes or until liquid is almost absorbed.

4 servings (about 1¼ cups each)

*1 can (16 ounces) black-eyed peas, drained, can be substituted for the frozen black-eyed peas. Do not precook.

Per Serving			
Calories	215	Fat	1 g
Protein	9 g	Unsaturated	1 g
Carbohydrate	44 g	Saturated	0 g
Sodium	610 mg	Cholesterol	0 mg

Hearty Bean and Pasta Stew

1 cup coarsely chopped tomato (about 1 large)
¾ cup uncooked macaroni shells
¼ cup chopped onion (about 1 small)
¼ cup chopped green bell pepper
1 tablespoon chopped fresh or 1 teaspoon dried basil
1 teaspoon Worcestershire sauce
1 clove garlic, finely chopped
1 can (16 ounces) kidney beans, drained
1 can (14½ ounces) chicken broth
1 can (8 ounces) garbanzo beans, drained

Mix all ingredients in 2-quart saucepan. Heat to boiling, stirring occasionally; reduce heat. Cover and simmer about 15 minutes, stirring occasionally, until macaroni is tender.

4 servings (about 1 cup each)

Per Serving			
Calories	220	Fat	2 g
Protein	11 g	Unsaturated	2 g
Carbohydrate	40 g	Saturated	0 g
Sodium	720 mg	Cholesterol	0 mg

Hearty Bean and Pasta Stew, Bean Patties (page 135)

Pita Pizzas

4 whole wheat pita breads (4 inches in diameter)
¼ cup chopped onion (about 1 small)
1 small clove garlic, finely chopped
1 can (15½ ounces) great northern beans, drained and ¼ cup liquid reserved
2 tablespoons chopped fresh or 2 teaspoons dried basil
1 large tomato, seeded and cut into ¼-inch pieces
1 large green bell pepper, cut into 16 thin rings
1 cup shredded part-skim mozzarella cheese (4 ounces)

Heat oven to 425°. Cut each pita bread around edge in half with knife. Place in ungreased jelly roll pan, 15½ × 10½ × 1 inch. Bake uncovered about 5 minutes or just until crisp. Cook onion and garlic in reserved bean liquid in 10-inch nonstick skillet over medium heat about 5 minutes, stirring occasionally. Stir in beans; heat through.

Place bean mixture and basil in blender or food processor. Cover and blend or process until smooth. Spread about 2 tablespoons bean mixture on each pita bread half. Top each with tomato, bell pepper and cheese. Bake in jelly roll pan 5 to 7 minutes or until cheese is melted.

4 servings

Per Serving			
Calories	415	Fat	7 g
Protein	23 g	Unsaturated	3 g
Carbohydrate	70 g	Saturated	4 g
Sodium	420 mg	Cholesterol	20 mg

Bean Patties

Yogurt sparked with horseradish makes an ideal accompaniment to this stand-in for the ubiquitous hamburger.

1 can (16 ounces) pinto beans, rinsed and well drained
½ cup shredded lowfat Cheddar cheese (2 ounces)
¼ cup dry bread crumbs
2 tablespoons chopped green onions (with tops)
1 teaspoon Worcestershire sauce
¼ teaspoon pepper
⅛ teaspoon salt
1 egg white or 2 tablespoons cholesterol-free egg product
4 whole wheat hamburger buns, split
Horseradish Sauce (below)
4 slices tomato
4 lettuce leaves

Spray 10-inch nonstick skillet with nonstick cooking spray. Mash beans in medium bowl. Mix in cheese, bread crumbs, onions, Worcestershire sauce, pepper, salt and egg white. Shape into 4 patties. Cook in skillet over medium heat about 10 minutes, turning once, until light brown. Serve on buns with Horseradish Sauce, tomato and lettuce.

4 servings

HORSERADISH SAUCE

½ cup plain nonfat yogurt
2 teaspoons prepared horseradish

Mix yogurt and horseradish.

Per Serving			
Calories	280	Fat	5 g
Protein	14 g	Unsaturated	3 g
Carbohydrate	42 g	Saturated	2 g
Sodium	790 mg	Cholesterol	0 mg

Enchilada Torta

This stacked bean and tortilla dish is perfect for making in the microwave.

1 cup refried beans
1 can (4 ounces) chopped green chilies
½ cup chopped tomato (about 1 small)
4 corn tortillas (6 inches in diameter)
1¼ cups Salsa Verde (page 170) or green sauce
1½ cups shredded lowfat Cheddar cheese (6 ounces)

Heat oven to 350°. Spray pie plate, 9 × 1¼ inches, with nonstick cooking spray. Mix beans, chilies and tomato. Place 1 tortilla in pie plate. Layer with ¼ of the bean mixture, Salsa Verde and cheese. Repeat 3 times. Cover loosely with aluminum foil. Bake 25 to 30 minutes or until cheese is melted and beans are heated through. Serve with low-fat sour cream if desired.

4 servings

MICROWAVE DIRECTIONS: prepare as directed—except use microwavable pie plate, 9 × 1¼ inches. Cover tightly and microwave on high 6 to 8 minutes, rotating pie plate ½ turn after 3 minutes, until center is hot and cheese is melted.

Per Serving			
Calories	325	Fat	11 g
Protein	19 g	Unsaturated	6 g
Carbohydrate	36 g	Saturated	5 g
Sodium	790 mg	Cholesterol	0 mg

Mexican Bean Bake

1 cup variety baking mix
¼ cup salsa
1 can (16 ounces) refried beans
1 can (4 ounces) chopped green chilies, undrained
¾ cup salsa
¾ cup shredded lowfat Cheddar cheese (3 ounces)
1 cup shredded lettuce
½ cup chopped tomato (about 1 small)
¼ cup plain nonfat yogurt

Heat oven to 375°. Spray square baking dish, 8 × 8 × 2 inches, with nonstick cooking spray. Mix baking mix, ¼ cup salsa, the beans and chilies. Spread in dish. Top with ¾ cup salsa and the cheese. Bake uncovered about 30 minutes or until set. Let stand 5 minutes before cutting. Top with lettuce, tomato and yogurt.

4 servings

Per Serving			
Calories	355	Fat	10 g
Protein	17 g	Unsaturated	7 g
Carbohydrate	49 g	Saturated	3 g
Sodium	1,320 mg	Cholesterol	0 mg

Curried Lentils and Barley

2 teaspoons vegetable oil
½ cup chopped onion (about 1 medium)
⅓ cup coarsely chopped red or green bell pepper
3½ cups water
½ cup uncooked barley
1½ teaspoons curry powder
¾ teaspoon salt
1 cup thinly sliced carrots (about 2 small)
¾ cup dried lentils, sorted and rinsed
½ cup plain nonfat yogurt
¼ cup chutney

Heat oil in 3-quart saucepan over medium-high heat. Sauté onion and bell pepper in oil. Stir in water, barley, curry powder and salt. Heat to boiling; reduce heat. Cover and simmer 15 minutes. Stir in carrots and lentils. Heat to boiling; reduce heat. Cover and simmer 40 to 45 minutes, stirring occasionally, until lentils are tender and liquid is absorbed. Mix yogurt and chutney. Serve with lentils and barley topped with yogurt mixture.

4 servings (about 1 cup each)

Per Serving			
Calories	315	Fat	3 g
Protein	14 g	Unsaturated	3 g
Carbohydrate	58 g	Saturated	0 g
Sodium	470 mg	Cholesterol	0 mg

Lentil Stew

2 teaspoons vegetable oil
1 cup chopped onions (about 2 medium)
1 clove garlic, finely chopped
3 cups water
2 cups coarsely chopped potatoes (about 2 medium)
1 cup dried lentils, sorted and rinsed
¼ cup chopped fresh parsley
½ teaspoon ground cumin
½ teaspoon salt
¼ teaspoon pepper
¼ teaspoon ground mace
8 ounces small fresh mushrooms, cut in half
1 can (28 ounces) whole tomatoes, undrained

Heat oil in Dutch oven over medium-high heat. Sauté onions and garlic in oil. Stir in remaining ingredients; break up tomatoes. Heat to boiling; reduce heat. Cover and simmer about 40 minutes, stirring occasionally, until potatoes are tender.

6 servings (about 1⅓ cups each)

Per Serving			
Calories	195	Fat	2 g
Protein	10 g	Unsaturated	2 g
Carbohydrate	37 g	Saturated	<1 g
Sodium	400 mg	Cholesterol	0 mg

Black Bean Salad

Chili Dressing (below)
1 cup frozen whole kernel corn, thawed
1 cup diced jicama
¾ cup chopped seeded tomato (about 1 medium)
2 green onions (with tops), sliced
2 cans (15 ounces each) black beans, rinsed and drained

Toss all ingredients in large glass or plastic bowl. Cover and refrigerate at least 2 hours, stirring occasionally.

4 servings (about 1 cup each)

CHILI DRESSING

¼ cup red wine vinegar
2 tablespoons vegetable oil
½ teaspoon chili powder
¼ teaspoon ground cumin
1 small clove garlic, crushed

Mix all ingredients.

Per Serving			
Calories	210	Fat	8 g
Protein	8 g	Unsaturated	7 g
Carbohydrate	30 g	Saturated	1 g
Sodium	30 mg	Cholesterol	0 mg

Wheat Berry Salad

Wheat berries are whole grains of wheat, and can be found in health food stores.

1 cup uncooked wheat berries
2½ cups water
1½ cups broccoli flowerets
½ cup chopped green onions (with tops)
½ cup diced carrot (about 1 medium)
1 can (15 ounces) garbanzo beans, drained
Vinaigrette Dressing (below)

Heat wheat berries and water to boiling in 2-quart saucepan, stirring once or twice; reduce heat. Cover and simmer 50 to 60 minutes or until wheat berries are tender but still firm; drain. Toss wheat berries and remaining ingredients. Cover and refrigerate at least 1 hour.

4 servings (about 1⅓ cups each)

VINAIGRETTE DRESSING

¼ cup balsamic or cider vinegar
2 tablespoons olive or vegetable oil
1 tablespoon chopped fresh or 1 teaspoon dried basil
¼ teaspoon paprika
⅛ teaspoon salt
1 clove garlic, crushed

Shake all ingredients in tightly covered container

Per Serving			
Calories	280	Fat	8 g
Protein	8 g	Unsaturated	7 g
Carbohydrate	46 g	Saturated	1 g
Sodium	300 mg	Cholesterol	0 mg

Black Bean Salad (bottom), Wheat Berry Salad (top)

Chapter 6

Breads, Sides and Accompaniments

- ◆ Many breads, eaten by themselves, are not high in fat. It's what we put on them that gets us into trouble.

- ◆ Toast is terrific with just a little jam or jelly. If you must have a spread, use reduced-calorie margarine.

- ◆ Pancakes really don't need margarine or butter at all. Just stack them up and enjoy with fresh fruit, preserves or a little syrup.

- ◆ Use chopped or pureed fruits and vegetables to add flavor and tenderness to breads—while decreasing fats.

- ◆ Take advantage of fruits and vegetables in season. Although many are available year-round, they are least expensive when grown locally. It's hard to beat the flavor and freshness of produce from your local farmer's market.

- ◆ Use nonstick cooking spray when cooking vegetables.

- ◆ Fresh herbs and spices are superb in the place of rich sauces. The low-fat White Sauce on page 166 can be the basis of many wonderful, homemade, creamy sauces.

- ◆ Use strongly flavored ingredients when making your salad dressings and you can reduce the oil drastically—or altogether. Balsamic vinegar, herb and fruit vinegars, peppercorns, chilies and fresh herbs all make for memorable vinaigrettes.

- ◆ The dressings and sauces on the pages that follow are delicious ways to perk up plain meats and vegetables.

Two-Pear Waldorf Salad (page 158), Spicy Apple-Bran Muffins (page 145)

Sour Cream Biscuits

Space biscuits about 1 inch apart for crusty biscuits, with sides touching for softer ones.

1¾ cups all-purpose flour
2½ teaspoons baking powder
¼ teaspoon salt
2 tablespoons firm margarine
½ cup lowfat sour cream
⅓ cup skim milk

Heat oven to 450°. Mix flour, baking powder and salt in large bowl. Cut in margarine with pastry blender until mixture resembles fine crumbs. Mix sour cream and milk until smooth. Stir sour cream mixture into flour mixture until dough leaves side of bowl.

Turn dough onto lightly floured surface. Knead lightly 10 times. Roll or pat ½ inch thick. Cut with floured 2½-inch round cutter. Place on ungreased cookie sheet. Bake 10 to 12 minutes or until golden brown.

8 biscuits

Per Biscuit			
Calories	130	Fat	4 g
Protein	3 g	Unsaturated	3 g
Carbohydrate	20 g	Saturated	1 g
Sodium	240 mg	Cholesterol	5 mg

Whole Wheat Blueberry Waffles

2 cups buttermilk
1 cup whole wheat flour
1 cup all-purpose flour
1 tablespoon sugar
3 tablespoons vegetable oil
2 teaspoons baking powder
1 teaspoon grated orange peel
¼ teaspoon salt
3 egg whites or ½ cup cholesterol-free egg product
1 cup fresh or frozen (thawed and drained) blueberries

Heat waffle iron; brush lightly with oil if necessary. Beat all ingredients except blueberries just until smooth. Stir in blueberries. Pour batter from cup or pitcher onto hot waffle iron. Bake about 5 minutes or until steaming stops. Remove waffle carefully.

Twelve 4-inch waffle squares

Per Waffle Square			
Calories	130	Fat	4 g
Protein	4 g	Unsaturated	3 g
Carbohydrate	19 g	Saturated	1 g
Sodium	170 mg	Cholesterol	0 mg

Whole Wheat Blueberry Waffles

Citrus-Currant Scones

Scones were originally cooked on a griddle but to-day, most are oven-baked. The dough can be patted into a circle and cut into wedges, as below, or cut out with biscuit or cookie cutters into shapes.

¼ cup sugar
2 teaspoons grated lemon or orange peel
1¾ cups all-purpose flour
2½ teaspoons baking powder
¼ teaspoon salt
3 tablespoons margarine
⅓ cup plain lowfat yogurt
3 egg whites, slightly beaten
½ cup currants or raisins
Skim milk

Heat oven to 375°. Mix sugar and lemon peel; reserve 1 tablespoon. Mix remaining sugar mixture, the flour, baking powder and salt in large bowl. Cut in margarine with pastry blender until mixture resembles fine crumbs. Stir in yogurt, egg whites and currants just until dough leaves side of bowl.

Turn dough onto lightly floured surface. Knead lightly 10 times. Place on ungreased cookie sheet. Pat into 8-inch circle, using floured hands. Cut circle into 12 wedges with sharp knife dipped in flour; do not separate wedges. Brush with milk. Sprinkle with reserved sugar mixture. Bake 18 to 20 minutes or until edges are light brown. Immediately remove from cookie sheet; cool.

12 scones

Per Scone			
Calories	125	Fat	3 g
Protein	3 g	Unsaturated	2 g
Carbohydrate	22 g	Saturated	1 g
Sodium	180 mg	Cholesterol	0 mg

Basil–Red Pepper Muffins

1 cup skim milk
⅓ cup olive oil
2 egg whites or ¼ cup cholesterol-free egg product
2 cups all-purpose flour
⅓ cup chopped red bell pepper
¼ cup chopped green onions (with tops)
2 tablespoons chopped fresh or 1 teaspoon dried basil
1 tablespoon sugar
3 teaspoons baking powder
½ teaspoon salt
⅛ teaspoon pepper

Heat oven to 400°. Spray 12 medium muffin cups, 2½ × 1¼ inches, with nonstick cooking spray. Beat milk, oil and egg whites in large bowl, using fork. Stir in remaining ingredients just until flour is moistened. Divide batter among muffin cups. Bake 18 to 20 minutes or until golden brown. Immediately remove muffins from pan.

12 muffins

MICROWAVE DIRECTIONS: Place 6 paper baking cups in microwavable muffin ring. Prepare batter as directed. Fill each muffin cup with scant ¼ cup batter. Microwave uncovered on high 3 to 5 minutes, rotating ring ¼ turn every minute, until tops are almost dry and wooden pick inserted in centers comes out clean. (Parts of muffins may appear slightly moist but will continue to cook while standing.) Immediately remove muffins from ring. Let stand uncovered on wire rack 2 minutes. Repeat with remaining batter.

Per Muffin			
Calories	140	Fat	6 g
Protein	3 g	Unsaturated	5 g
Carbohydrate	17 g	Saturated	1 g
Sodium	210 mg	Cholesterol	0 mg

Spicy Apple-Bran Muffins

Using yogurt means you can reduce the amount of oil in muffins and still get a tender texture. To save on a few extra calories, omit the brown sugar topping.

1 cup plain nonfat yogurt
1 cup chopped apple (about 1 medium)
¼ cup frozen (thawed) apple juice concentrate
¼ cup Egg Substitute (page 116) or cholesterol-free egg product
3 tablespoons vegetable oil
1 cup oat bran
1 cup all-purpose flour
¼ cup granulated sugar
3 teaspoons baking powder
¾ teaspoon ground cinnamon
¼ teaspoon salt
¼ teaspoon ground nutmeg
1 tablespoon packed brown sugar

Heat oven to 400°. Spray 12 medium muffin cups, 2½ × 1¼ inches, with nonstick cooking spray or line with paper baking cups. Mix yogurt, apple, apple juice concentrate, Egg Substitute and oil in large bowl until blended. Stir in remaining ingredients except brown sugar all at once just until flour is moistened. Fill muffin cups about ⅞ full. Sprinkle with brown sugar. Bake 20 to 24 minutes or until golden brown. Immediately remove from pan.

12 muffins

Per Muffin			
Calories	105	Fat	4 g
Protein	4 g	Unsaturated	3 g
Carbohydrate	20 g	Saturated	<1 g
Sodium	170 mg	Cholesterol	0 mg

Parmesan-Pepper Rolls

2¼ cups all-purpose flour
2 tablespoons sugar
2 tablespoons grated Parmesan cheese
1 teaspoon salt
¼ teaspoon coarsely ground pepper
1 package active dry yeast
1 cup very warm water (120° to 130°)
2 egg whites or ¼ cup cholesterol-free egg product
2 tablespoons vegetable oil

Mix 1¼ cups of the flour, the sugar, cheese, salt, pepper and yeast in large bowl. Beat in water, egg whites and oil until smooth. Stir in remaining flour until smooth. Scrape batter from side of bowl. Cover and let rise in warm place about 30 minutes or until double.

Spray 12 medium muffin cups, 2½ × 1¼ inches, with nonstick cooking spray. Stir down batter, beating about 25 strokes. Divide batter among muffin cups. Let rise uncovered 20 to 30 minutes or until batter rounds over tops of cups.

Heat oven to 400°. Bake 15 to 20 minutes or until golden brown.

12 rolls

Per Roll			
Calories	115	Fat	3 g
Protein	3 g	Unsaturated	2 g
Carbohydrate	19 g	Saturated	1 g
Sodium	210 mg	Cholesterol	0 mg

Fresh Pear Coffee Cake

¾ cup sugar
¼ cup margarine, softened
1 teaspoon vanilla
3 egg whites or ½ cup cholesterol-free egg product
1¾ cups all-purpose flour
1 teaspoon baking powder
½ teaspoon baking soda
½ teaspoon ground cardamom
¼ teaspoon salt
1 cup lowfat sour cream
2 cups chopped unpared pears (about 2 medium)
Streusel (right)
Glaze (right)

Heat oven to 350°. With nonstick cooking spray, spray rectangular pan, 13 × 9 × 2 inches. Beat sugar, margarine, vanilla and egg whites in large bowl on medium speed 2 minutes, scraping bowl occasionally. Mix flour, baking powder, baking soda, cardamom and salt; beat into sugar mixture alternately with sour cream on low speed. Fold in pears. Spread batter in pan. Sprinkle with Streusel. Bake 45 to 55 minutes or until wooden pick inserted in center comes out clean; cool. Drizzle with Glaze.

15 servings

STREUSEL

⅓ cup granulated sugar
⅓ cup packed brown sugar
2 tablespoons all-purpose flour
½ teaspoon ground cinnamon
2 tablespoons firm margarine

Mix sugars, flour and cinnamon. Cut in margarine until crumbly.

GLAZE

½ cup powdered sugar
2 to 3 teaspoons skim milk
¼ teaspoon vanilla

Mix all ingredients until smooth.

Per Serving			
Calories	210	Fat	5 g
Protein	3 g	Unsaturated	4 g
Carbohydrate	38 g	Saturated	1 g
Sodium	210 mg	Cholesterol	5 mg

Fresh Pear Coffee Cake, Easy Multigrain Bread (page 149)

Zucchini-Apricot Bread

1½ cups shredded zucchini (about 1 medium)
¾ cup sugar
¼ cup vegetable oil
3 egg whites or ½ cup cholesterol-free egg product
1½ cups all-purpose flour
1 teaspoon ground cinnamon
2 teaspoons vanilla
¾ teaspoon baking soda
½ teaspoon salt
¼ teaspoon baking powder
¼ teaspoon ground cloves
½ cup finely chopped dried apricots

Heat oven to 350°. Spray loaf pan, 9 × 5 × 3 or 8½ × 4½ × 2½ inches, with nonstick cooking spray. Mix zucchini, sugar, oil and egg whites in large bowl. Stir in remaining ingredients except apricots. Stir in apricots. Pour into pan. Bake 60 to 70 minutes or until wooden pick inserted in center comes out clean. Cool 10 minutes. Loosen sides of loaf from pan; remove from pan. Cool completely before slicing.

1 loaf (24 slices)

Per Slice			
Calories	85	Fat	2 g
Protein	1 g	Unsaturated	2 g
Carbohydrate	14 g	Saturated	0 g
Sodium	90 mg	Cholesterol	0 mg

Pumpkin-Fruit Bread

The ring mold used in the microwave variation allows for even baking, and cornflake crumbs give the exterior a tempting "crust."

1 cup canned pumpkin
⅔ cup packed brown sugar
3 tablespoons vegetable oil
1 teaspoon vanilla
3 egg whites or ½ cup cholesterol-free egg product
1½ cups all-purpose flour
1 teaspoon baking soda
¾ teaspoon ground cinnamon
½ teaspoon salt
¼ teaspoon ground cloves
¼ teaspoon baking powder
½ cup chopped mixed dried fruit

Heat oven to 350°. Spray loaf pan, 9 × 5 × 3 or 8½ × 4½ × 2½ inches, with nonstick cooking spray. Mix pumpkin, brown sugar, oil, vanilla and egg whites in large bowl. Stir in remaining ingredients except fruit just until moistened. Stir in fruit. Pour into pan. Bake 50 to 60 minutes or until wooden pick inserted in center comes out clean. Cool 5 minutes. Loosen sides of loaf from pan; remove from pan. Cool completely before slicing.

1 loaf (24 slices)

MICROWAVE DIRECTIONS: Spray 6-cup microwavable ring dish generously with nonstick cooking spray. Coat with 2 tablespoons cornflake crumbs. Prepare batter as directed. Spoon into ring dish; spread evenly. Microwave uncovered on medium-high (70%) 8 to 10 minutes, rotating dish ¼ turn every 3 minutes, until wooden pick inserted near center comes out clean. Cool 5 minutes on heatproof surface (do not use rack).

Per Slice			
Calories	80	Fat	2 g
Protein	1 g	Unsaturated	1 g
Carbohydrate	15 g	Saturated	<1 g
Sodium	60 mg	Cholesterol	0 mg

Easy Multigrain Bread

Using multigrain hot cereal is a shortcut to keeping several different flours on hand for breadmaking.

1 package active dry yeast
1¼ cups warm water (105° to 115°)
2 cups all-purpose flour
2 tablespoons honey
2 tablespoons margarine, softened
1 teaspoon salt
1 cup whole wheat flour
½ cup uncooked mixed grain hot cereal (dry)

Dissolve yeast in warm water in large bowl. Add all-purpose flour, honey, margarine and salt. Beat on low speed 30 seconds, scraping bowl constantly. Beat on medium speed 2 minutes, scraping bowl occasionally (or beat 300 vigorous strokes by hand). Stir in whole wheat flour and cereal until well blended. Scrape batter from side of bowl. Cover and let rise in warm place 40 to 45 minutes or until almost double.

Spray loaf pan, 9 × 5 × 3 or 8½ × 4½ × 2½ inches, with nonstick cooking spray. Stir down batter by beating about 25 strokes. Spread batter in pan. Smooth and pat batter, using floured hand. Cover and let rise in warm place about 30 minutes or until double. (Batter is ready if indentation remains when touched with floured finger.)

Heat oven to 375°. Bake 35 to 40 minutes or until loaf sounds hollow when tapped. Remove loaf from pan; cool on wire rack.

1 loaf (20 slices)

Per Slice			
Calories	80	Fat	1 g
Protein	2 g	Unsaturated	1 g
Carbohydrate	15 g	Saturated	0 g
Sodium	125 mg	Cholesterol	0 mg

Tangy Carrots with Grapes

2 cups thin diagonal slices carrots (about 4 medium)
1 shallot, chopped
¼ cup water
2 tablespoons balsamic or red wine vinegar
1 tablespoon packed brown sugar
½ cup seedless grape halves

Cook carrots and shallot in water in 10-inch nonstick skillet over medium heat 8 to 10 minutes, stirring occasionally, until water is evaporated and carrots are tender. Push carrot mixture to side of skillet. Stir in vinegar and brown sugar. Add grapes. Toss carrots, grapes and vinegar mixture.

4 servings (about ½ cup each)

MICROWAVE DIRECTIONS: Decrease vinegar to 1 tablespoon. Place carrots, shallot and water in 1½-quart microwavable casserole. Cover tightly and microwave on high 5 to 8 minutes, stirring after 3 minutes, until carrots are crisp-tender; drain. Add vinegar and brown sugar; toss. Stir in grapes. Cover tightly and microwave 1 minute or until heated through.

Per Serving			
Calories	65	Fat	0 g
Protein	1 g	Unsaturated	0 g
Carbohydrate	16 g	Saturated	0 g
Sodium	30 mg	Cholesterol	0 mg

Skillet Okra and Rice

1 teaspoon vegetable oil
⅓ cup uncooked regular long grain rice
¼ cup chopped onion (about 1 small)
¼ cup chopped green bell pepper
1 small clove garlic, finely chopped
1 cup chopped tomato (about 1 large)
⅔ cup chicken broth
½ teaspoon chopped fresh or ⅛ teaspoon dried thyme
¼ teaspoon pepper
⅛ teaspoon red pepper sauce
1 small bay leaf
*8 ounces okra, cut into ½-inch slices**

Heat oil in 10-inch nonstick skillet over medium-high heat. Sauté rice in oil about 3 minutes or until golden brown. Stir in onion, bell pepper and garlic. Sauté about 5 minutes until onion begins to soften. Stir in remaining ingredients except okra. Heat to boiling; reduce heat. Cover and simmer until rice is tender. Stir in okra. Cover and simmer 10 minutes longer or until okra is tender. Remove bay leaf.

4 servings (about ½ cup each)

*1 package (10 ounces) frozen cut okra can be substituted for the fresh okra. Thaw just enough to separate.

Per Serving			
Calories	50	Fat	1 g
Protein	2 g	Unsaturated	1 g
Carbohydrate	8 g	Saturated	0 g
Sodium	75 mg	Cholesterol	0 mg

Sweet Potato-Apple Puree

Because yams are darker than sweet potatoes, they give this puree a more intense color. Try piping this puree into individual servings.

3 cups cubed pared sweet potatoes or yams
  (about 3 medium)
2 cups coarsely chopped pared cooking apples
  (about 2 medium)
1 tablespoon apple brandy
⅛ teaspoon salt

Heat ½ inch water to boiling. Add sweet potatoes and apples. Cover and heat to boiling; reduce heat. Boil 8 to 10 minutes or until tender; drain. Add brandy and salt; mash until desired consistency.

4 servings (about ⅔ cup each)

MICROWAVE DIRECTIONS: Place sweet potatoes, apples and ¼ cup water in 2-quart microwavable casserole. Cover tightly and microwave on high 10 to 12 minutes, stirring after 5 minutes, until sweet potatoes are tender. Let stand covered 2 minutes. Drain carefully. Add brandy and salt; mash until desired consistency.

Per Serving			
Calories	155	Fat	<1 g
Protein	2 g	Unsaturated	0 g
Carbohydrate	35 g	Saturated	0 g
Sodium	85 mg	Cholesterol	0 mg

Sweet Potato-Apple Puree

Sweet-and-Sour Cabbage with Plantain

Ripe plantains have black skins and are slightly soft.

¼ cup chicken broth
2 tablespoons packed brown sugar
2 tablespoons cider vinegar
2 teaspoons cornstarch
¼ teaspoon red pepper sauce
2 teaspoons vegetable oil
1 ripe medium plantain, cut into ¼-inch slices
⅓ cup sliced green onions (with tops)
¼ cup 1 × ⅛-inch strips red bell pepper
4 cups coarsely shredded savoy cabbage
  (about 1 small head)

Mix broth, brown sugar, vinegar, cornstarch and pepper sauce; reserve. Heat oil in 10-inch nonstick skillet over high heat. Add plantain, onions and bell pepper; stir-fry 1 minute. Add cabbage; stir-fry 2 minutes. Stir in cornstarch mixture; stir-fry 10 seconds or until thickened.

4 servings (about ¾ cup each)

Per Serving			
Calories	135	Fat	3 g
Protein	2 g	Unsaturated	2 g
Carbohydrate	28 g	Saturated	<1 g
Sodium	70 mg	Cholesterol	0 mg

Chili-Corn Pudding

1 tablespoon margarine
¼ cup chopped onion (about 1 small)
¼ cup chopped red bell pepper
2 tablespoons all-purpose flour
½ teaspoon salt
½ teaspoon chili powder
½ teaspoon ground cumin
¾ cup skim milk
2 cups cooked whole kernel corn
2 egg whites or ¼ cup cholesterol-free egg product
1 can (4 ounces) chopped green chilies, drained

Heat oven to 350°. Heat margarine in 2-quart saucepan over medium-high heat. Sauté onion and bell pepper in margarine; remove from heat. Stir in flour, salt, chili powder and cumin. Cook over medium heat, stirring constantly, until bubbly; remove from heat. Gradually stir in milk. Heat to boiling, stirring constantly. Boil and stir 1 minute. Stir in corn, egg whites and chilies. Pour into ungreased square baking dish, 8 × 8 × 2 inches. Bake uncovered 25 to 30 minutes or until bubbly. Garnish with red bell pepper rings if desired.

4 servings (about ¾ cup each)

Per Serving			
Calories	140	Fat	4 g
Protein	6 g	Unsaturated	3 g
Carbohydrate	23 g	Saturated	1 g
Sodium	360 mg	Cholesterol	0 mg

Sweet-and-Sour Cabbage with Plantain

Saucy Jerusalem Artichokes

Native to the Americas, the Jerusalem artichoke is a crisp, sweet root that resembles a somewhat watery potato. It's delicious raw, too, especially in salads.

1 pound Jerusalem artichokes, cut into ¼-inch slices
  (about 3½ cups)
1 cup skim milk
1 tablespoon cornstarch
1 tablespoon chopped fresh or 1 teaspoon freeze-dried
  chives
1 teaspoon chopped fresh or ½ teaspoon dried dill
  weed
¼ teaspoon salt
⅛ teaspoon pepper
3 ounces partskim Swiss cheese, shredded (¾ cup)

Place steamer basket in ½ inch water (water should not touch bottom of basket). Place artichokes in basket. Cover tightly and heat to boiling; reduce heat. Steam 10 to 12 minutes or until crisp-tender.

Mix remaining ingredients except cheese in 2-quart saucepan. Cook over medium heat, stirring constantly, until mixture thickens and boils. Boil and stir 1 minute; remove from heat. Stir in cheese until melted. Stir in artichokes.

4 servings (about ¾ cup each)

MICROWAVE DIRECTIONS: Place artichokes and ¼ cup water in 1½-quart microwavable casserole. Cover tightly and microwave on high 6 to 7 minutes, stirring after 3 minutes, until crisp-tender; drain. Mix remaining ingredients except cheese in 4-cup microwavable measure. Microwave uncovered on high 3 to 4 minutes, stirring every minute, until thickened. Stir in cheese until melted. Stir into artichokes.

Per Serving			
Calories	185	Fat	4 g
Protein	11 g	Unsaturated	1 g
Carbohydrate	26 g	Saturated	3 g
Sodium	210 mg	Cholesterol	15 mg

Leeks au Gratin

4 medium leeks with tops (about 2 pounds), cut into
  ½-inch pieces
Crumb Topping (below)
1 tablespoon margarine
1 tablespoon plus 1 teaspoon all-purpose flour
¼ teaspoon salt
Dash of pepper
⅔ cup skim milk
½ cup shredded Gruyère cheese (2 ounces)

Heat 1 inch water to boiling. Add leeks. Cover and cook over medium heat about 5 minutes or until crisp-tender; drain.

Heat oven to 325°. Prepare Crumb Topping. Spray shallow 1-quart casserole with nonstick cooking spray. Heat margarine in 2-quart saucepan over low heat. Stir in flour, salt and pepper. Cook over low heat, stirring constantly, until margarine is absorbed; remove from heat. Gradually stir in milk. Heat to boiling, stirring constantly. Boil and stir 1 minute. Stir in cheese until melted. Stir in leeks. Pour into casserole. Sprinkle with Crumb Topping. Bake uncovered about 25 minutes or until heated through.

4 servings (about ½ cup each)

CRUMB TOPPING

Mix 2 tablespoons dry bread crumbs and 1 teaspoon margarine, melted.

Per Serving			
Calories	255	Fat	8 g
Protein	10 g	Unsaturated	5 g
Carbohydrate	38 g	Saturated	3 g
Sodium	310 mg	Cholesterol	15 mg

Leeks au Gratin

Oriental Coleslaw

2 cups finely shredded Chinese cabbage (about ½ pound)
¼ cup chopped jicama
¼ cup chopped green bell pepper
¼ cup coarsely shredded carrot
Sesame Dressing (below)

Toss all ingredients.

4 servings (about ¾ cup each)

SESAME DRESSING

3 tablespoons rice or white wine vinegar
2 teaspoons sugar
2 teaspoons sesame seed, toasted
2 teaspoons low-sodium soy sauce
1 teaspoon sesame oil
⅛ teaspoon crushed red pepper

Mix all ingredients.

Per Serving			
Calories	45	Fat	2 g
Protein	1 g	Unsaturated	2 g
Carbohydrate	6 g	Saturated	<1 g
Sodium	145 mg	Cholesterol	0 mg

Zesty Fruit Salad

1 cup strawberries, cut in half
1 medium papaya, peeled, seeded and cut into 1-inch
  pieces (about 2 cups)
1 kiwifruit, pared and thinly sliced
1 starfruit, thinly sliced and seeded
Jalapeño Dressing (below)

Toss all ingredients. Serve on salad greens if desired.

4 servings (about 1 cup each)

JALAPEÑO DRESSING

1 tablespoon chopped fresh cilantro
1 tablespoon vegetable oil
1 tablespoon lime juice
1 teaspoon sugar
½ small jalapeño chili, seeded and very finely chopped

Mix all ingredients.

Per Serving			
Calories	105	Fat	4 g
Protein	1 g	Unsaturated	3 g
Carbohydrate	17 g	Saturated	<1 g
Sodium	5 mg	Cholesterol	0 mg

Oriental Coleslaw

Two-Pear Waldorf Salad

The most common variety of Asian pear is large, round, yellow-green and sweeter and crunchier than an ordinary pear. If Asian pears aren't to be found, substitute an apple or another Bosc pear.

⅓ cup plain lowfat yogurt
1 tablespoon cholesterol-free reduced-calorie mayonnaise or salad dressing
½ teaspoon finely grated lime peel
1 teaspoon lime juice
½ cup sliced celery (about 1 stalk)
½ cup seedless red grape halves
2 tablespoons chopped walnuts
1 Bosc or Anjou pear, coarsely chopped
1 Asian pear, coarsely chopped

Mix yogurt, mayonnaise, lime peel and lime juice. Toss with remaining ingredients.

4 servings (about ¾ cup each)

Per Serving			
Calories	105	Fat	4 g
Protein	2 g	Unsaturated	3 g
Carbohydrate	18 g	Saturated	1 g
Sodium	50 mg	Cholesterol	1 mg

Marinated Fennel and Pepper Salad

Italian Dressing (below)
1 medium fennel bulb (about 5 ounces)
1 cup sliced fresh mushrooms (about 3 ounces)
1 cup ½-inch slices zucchini (about 1 small)
½ cup coarsely chopped red bell pepper (about 1 small)

Prepare Italian Dressing. Cut fennel bulb lengthwise in half; cut halves crosswise into thin slices. Mix fennel, dressing and remaining ingredients in large glass or plastic bowl. Cover and refrigerate at least 4 hours, stirring occasionally.

4 servings (about 1 cup each)

ITALIAN DRESSING

3 tablespoons olive or vegetable oil
3 tablespoons red wine vinegar
3 tablespoons water
1 tablespoon finely chopped onion
1 teaspoon chopped fresh or ¼ teaspoon dried basil
1 teaspoon chopped fresh or ¼ teaspoon dried oregano
¼ teaspoon salt
¼ teaspoon sugar
¼ teaspoon dry mustard
1 small clove garlic, finely chopped

Shake all ingredients in tightly covered container.

Per Serving			
Calories	55	Fat	4 g
Protein	1 g	Unsaturated	3 g
Carbohydrate	4 g	Saturated	<1 g
Sodium	55 mg	Cholesterol	0 mg

Italian Pasta Salad

1 cup uncooked spiral macaroni
2 cups bite-size pieces salad greens
½ cup sliced cauliflowerets
½ cup broccoli flowerets
⅓ cup Parmesan Dressing (page 162)
¼ cup sliced zucchini
3 tablespoons sliced green onions (with tops)
2 tablespoons sliced ripe olives
1 small tomato, cut into wedges

Cook macaroni as directed on package. Rinse with cold water until cool; drain. Toss with remaining ingredients. Serve with freshly cracked black pepper if desired.

4 servings (about 1½ cups each)

Per Serving			
Calories	145	Fat	2 g
Protein	6 g	Unsaturated	1 g
Carbohydrate	27 g	Saturated	<1 g
Sodium	115 mg	Cholesterol	0 mg

Two-Potato Salad with Dill Dressing

½ cup plain nonfat yogurt
1 tablespoon cholesterol-free reduced-calorie mayonnaise or salad dressing
1 teaspoon chopped fresh or ½ teaspoon dried dill weed
1 teaspoon Dijon mustard
¼ teaspoon salt
2 cups cubed cooked white potato (about 1 large)
2 cups cubed cooked sweet potato or yam (about 1 large)
⅓ cup chopped celery (about 1 small stalk)
¼ cup sliced radishes
2 tablespoons chopped green onions (with tops)

Mix yogurt, mayonnaise, dill weed, mustard and salt in large glass or plastic bowl. Toss with remaining ingredients. Cover and refrigerate about 4 hours or until chilled.

4 servings (about 1 cup each)

Per Serving			
Calories	150	Fat	2 g
Protein	4 g	Unsaturated	1 g
Carbohydrate	29 g	Saturated	<1 g
Sodium	230 mg	Cholesterol	0 mg

Creamy Herb Dressing

Try this as a dip with vegetables, or to sauce cold poached chicken or fish.

1 cup plain nonfat yogurt
¾ cup buttermilk
¼ cup cholesterol-free reduced-calorie mayonnaise or salad dressing
2 tablespoons chopped green onions (with tops)
1 tablespoon chopped fresh parsley
2 teaspoons chopped fresh or ½ teaspoon dried dill weed
½ teaspoon Worcestershire sauce
¼ teaspoon salt
1 clove garlic, crushed
Dash of freshly ground pepper

Mix all ingredients. Cover and refrigerate any remaining dressing.

About 2 cups dressing

Per Tablespoon			
Calories	13	Fat	1 g
Protein	1 g	Unsaturated	<1 g
Carbohydrate	1 g	Saturated	0 g
Sodium	45 mg	Cholesterol	0 mg

Warm Greens with Balsamic Vinaigrette

¼ cup Balsamic Vinaigrette (page 162)
1½ cups sliced fresh mushrooms (about 4 ounces)
2 cups 2-inch pieces leaf lettuce
2 cups 2-inch pieces spinach
1½ cups 2-inch pieces radicchio
2 tablespoons pine nuts, toasted

Heat Balsamic Vinaigrette in 10-inch skillet over medium heat. Cook mushrooms in vinaigrette 3 minutes; remove from heat. Add remaining ingredients. Toss 1 to 2 minutes or until greens begin to wilt. Serve immediately. Sprinkle with freshly ground pepper if desired.

4 servings (about 1 cup each)

Per Serving			
Calories	75	Fat	6 g
Protein	2 g	Unsaturated	5 g
Carbohydrate	5 g	Saturated	1 g
Sodium	65 mg	Cholesterol	0 mg

Warm Greens with Balsamic Vinaigrette, Salmon with Dilled Cucumbers (page 98)

Parmesan Dressing

1 cup plain nonfat yogurt
¼ cup grated Parmesan cheese
⅓ cup skim milk
¼ teaspoon paprika
⅛ teaspoon salt
1 small clove garlic, finely chopped

Mix all ingredients. Cover and refrigerate any remaining dressing.

About 1½ cups dressing

Per Tablespoon			
Calories	10	Fat	0 g
Protein	1 g	Unsaturated	0 g
Carbohydrate	1 g	Saturated	0 g
Sodium	35 mg	Cholesterol	0 mg

Balsamic Vinaigrette

The characteristically rich flavor and aroma of Italian balsamic vinegar are due in part to aging in wooden casks for several years.

⅓ cup water
¼ cup balsamic vinegar
¼ cup olive oil
1 teaspoon honey
¼ teaspoon salt
¼ teaspoon paprika
1 clove garlic, crushed

Shake all ingredients in tightly covered container. Refrigerate at least 1 hour. Shake before serving.

About 1 cup dressing

Per Tablespoon			
Calories	30	Fat	3 g
Protein	0 g	Unsaturated	3 g
Carbohydrate	1 g	Saturated	0 g
Sodium	35 mg	Cholesterol	0 mg

Chipotle Dressing

Chipotles are smoked, dried jalapeño chilies. If they aren't available, half of a finely chopped, seeded jalapeño plus a dash of paprika and a drop of yellow food color can be used instead.

1 cup plain nonfat yogurt
¼ cup cholesterol-free reduced-calorie mayonnaise or salad dressing
2 tablespoons finely chopped canned chipotle chilies in adobo sauce
½ teaspoon ground cumin
¼ teaspoon salt

Beat all ingredients until smooth. Cover and refrigerate at least 2 hours.

About 1¼ cups dressing

Per Tablespoon			
Calories	10	Fat	1 g
Protein	0 g	Unsaturated	<1 g
Carbohydrate	1 g	Saturated	0 g
Sodium	50 mg	Cholesterol	0 mg

Raspberry-Peppercorn Dressing

Flavored vinegars can be found at many grocery stores and supermarkets. This dressing, with a sweet hint of raspberry, is delightful on any tossed green salad.

1 tablespoon sugar
2 teaspoons cornstarch
⅛ teaspoon salt
⅔ cup water
⅓ cup raspberry vinegar
1 tablespoon chopped fresh cilantro
1 to 2 teaspoons green peppercorns in water, drained*

Mix sugar, cornstarch and salt in 1-quart saucepan. Gradually stir in water and vinegar. Cook over medium heat, stirring constantly, until mixture thickens and boils. Boil and stir 1 minute; remove from heat. Stir in cilantro and peppercorns. Cover and refrigerate any remaining dressing.

About 1 cup dressing

*½ teaspoon coarsely ground black pepper can be substituted for the peppercorns.

Per Tablespoon			
Calories	5	Fat	0 g
Protein	0 g	Unsaturated	0 g
Carbohydrate	1 g	Saturated	0 g
Sodium	15 mg	Cholesterol	0 mg

Peach–Poppy Seed Vinaigrette

⅓ cup orange juice
2 tablespoons vegetable oil
2 tablespoons white wine vinegar
2 teaspoons honey
⅛ teaspoon salt
1 large peach, peeled and cut in half*
1 teaspoon poppy seed

Place all ingredients except poppy seed in blender or food processor. Cover and blend or process on medium speed until smooth. Stir in poppy seed. Cover and refrigerate at least 1 hour.

About 1¼ cups vinaigrette

*1 mango or large nectarine can be substituted for the peach.

Per Tablespoon			
Calories	20	Fat	1 g
Protein	0 g	Unsaturated	1 g
Carbohydrate	2 g	Saturated	0 g
Sodium	15 mg	Cholesterol	0 mg

Following pages: Chipotle Dressing (left), Parmesan Dressing (middle), Peach-Poppy Seed Vinaigrette (right)

White Sauce

This variation of basic white sauce, made with skim milk and half the usual amount of margarine, is a fine substitute. Use as a basic white sauce.

1 tablespoon margarine
2 tablespoons all-purpose flour
¼ teaspoon salt
⅛ teaspoon pepper
1 cup skim milk

Heat margarine in 1½-quart nonstick saucepan over low heat. Stir in flour, salt and pepper. Cook over low heat, stirring constantly, until margarine is absorbed; remove from heat. Gradually stir in milk. Heat to boiling, stirring constantly. Boil and stir 1 minute.

About 1 cup sauce

MICROWAVE DIRECTIONS: Place margarine in 4-cup microwavable measure. Microwave uncovered on high 15 to 20 seconds or until melted. Stir in flour, salt and pepper until margarine is absorbed. Gradually stir in milk. Microwave uncovered 3 to 4 minutes, stirring every minute, until thickened.

	Per Tablespoon		
Calories	15	Fat	1 g
Protein	1 g	Unsaturated	1 g
Carbohydrate	1 g	Saturated	0 g
Sodium	50 mg	Cholesterol	0 mg

Cheese Sauce

1 tablespoon margarine
2 tablespoons all-purpose flour
¼ teaspoon salt
¼ teaspoon dry mustard
⅛ teaspoon pepper
1 cup skim milk
1 cup shredded lowfat Cheddar cheese (4 ounces)

Heat margarine in 1½-quart nonstick saucepan over low heat. Stir in flour, salt, mustard and pepper. Cook over low heat, stirring constantly, until margarine is absorbed; remove from heat. Gradually stir in milk. Heat to boiling, stirring constantly. Boil and stir 1 minute. Stir in cheese until melted.

About 1⅓ cups sauce

MICROWAVE DIRECTIONS: Place margarine in 4-cup microwavable measure. Microwave uncovered on high 15 to 20 seconds or until melted. Stir in flour, salt, mustard and pepper until margarine is absorbed. Gradually stir in milk. Microwave uncovered 3 to 4 minutes, stirring every minute, until thickened. Stir in cheese until melted.

	Per Tablespoon		
Calories	20	Fat	1 g
Protein	1 g	Unsaturated	<1 g
Carbohydrate	1 g	Saturated	<1 g
Sodium	30 mg	Cholesterol	0 mg

Mushroom Sauce

1 tablespoon margarine
½ cup thinly sliced fresh mushrooms (about 1½ ounces)
2 tablespoons all-purpose flour
*½ teaspoon chopped fresh or ¼ teaspoon dried
    tarragon*
¼ teaspoon salt
⅛ teaspoon pepper
1 cup skim milk
1 tablespoon dry sherry

Heat margarine in 1½-quart nonstick saucepan over medium-high heat. Sauté mushrooms in margarine until liquid is evaporated. Stir in flour, tarragon, salt and pepper. Cook over low heat, stirring constantly, until margarine is absorbed; remove from heat. Gradually stir in milk. Heat to boiling, stirring constantly. Boil and stir 2 minutes. Stir in sherry.

About 1¼ cups sauce

MICROWAVE DIRECTIONS: Place margarine and mushrooms in 4-cup microwavable measure. Microwave uncovered on high 1 minute to 1 minute 30 seconds or until mushrooms are soft. Stir in flour, tarragon, salt and pepper until margarine is absorbed. Gradually stir in milk. Microwave uncovered 3 to 4 minutes, stirring every minute, until thickened. Stir in sherry.

Per Tablespoon			
Calories	15	Fat	1 g
Protein	1 g	Unsaturated	1 g
Carbohydrate	1 g	Saturated	0 g
Sodium	40 mg	Cholesterol	0 mg

Spinach-Herb Sauce

½ cup lightly packed fresh spinach
½ cup lightly packed fresh parsley
¼ cup lightly packed fresh sorrel
*1 cup cholesterol-free reduced-calorie mayonnaise or
    salad dressing*
½ cup plain nonfat yogurt

Place all ingredients in blender or food processor. Cover and blend or process until smooth. Cover and refrigerate about 1 hour or until chilled. Serve with cold poached salmon or shark.

About 1¾ cups sauce

Per Tablespoon			
Calories	30	Fat	3 g
Protein	0 g	Unsaturated	2 g
Carbohydrate	1 g	Saturated	>1 g
Sodium	75 mg	Cholesterol	0 mg

Orange Béarnaise Sauce

Serve this delicious mock béarnaise with chicken, fish or beef. It is thickened with cornstarch rather than egg yolks.

½ cup cold water
1 tablespoon cornstarch
¼ cup margarine
1 tablespoon orange juice
1 tablespoon finely chopped onion
1 teaspoon chopped fresh or ¼ teaspoon dried chervil
1 teaspoon chopped fresh or ¼ teaspoon dried tarragon
½ teaspoon grated orange peel
⅛ teaspoon salt
3 drops yellow food color
⅓ cup plain nonfat yogurt

Gradually stir water into cornstarch in 1-quart nonstick saucepan. Stir in remaining ingredients except yogurt. Heat over medium heat, stirring constantly, until mixture thickens and boils. Boil and stir 1 minute; remove from heat. Place yogurt in small bowl. Beat vigorously with fork until smooth. Pour hot mixture into yogurt, beating constantly with fork.

About 1 cup sauce

MICROWAVE DIRECTIONS: Decrease water by 1 tablespoon. Gradually stir water into cornstarch in 2-cup microwavable measure. Stir in remaining ingredients except yogurt. Microwave uncovered on high 2 minutes 30 seconds to 3 minutes 30 seconds, stirring ever minute, until thickened. Place yogurt in small bowl. Beat vigorously with fork until smooth. Pour hot mixture into yogurt, beating constantly with fork.

Per Tablespoon			
Calories	30	Fat	3 g
Protein	0 g	Unsaturated	2 g
Carbohydrate	1 g	Saturated	<1 g
Sodium	55 mg	Cholesterol	0 mg

Orange Béarnaise Sauce

Tartar Sauce

This low-fat tartar sauce is a wonderful accompaniment to fish, of course, but makes a great sandwich spread too.

1 cup cholesterol-free reduced-calorie mayonnaise or salad dressing
¼ cup finely chopped dill pickle
1 tablespoon chopped fresh parsley
1 tablespoon chopped green onion (with top)
2 teaspoons lemon juice
½ teaspoon Dijon mustard

Mix all ingredients. Cover and refrigerate about 1 hour or until chilled.

About 1¼ cups sauce

Per Tablespoon			
Calories	40	Fat	4 g
Protein	0 g	Unsaturated	3 g
Carbohydrate	1 g	Saturated	<1 g
Sodium	125 mg	Cholesterol	0 mg

Cucumber-Yogurt Sauce

½ cup plain nonfat yogurt
1 tablespoon chopped fresh or 1 teaspoon dried
  dill weed
1½ teaspoons chopped fresh mint
½ teaspoon Dijon mustard
⅛ teaspoon salt
1 large cucumber, pared, seeded, shredded and drained

Mix all ingredients. Cover and refrigerate about 1 hour or until chilled.

About 1¼ cups sauce

	Per Tablespoon		
Calories	5	Fat	0 g
Protein	0 g	Unsaturated	0 g
Carbohydrate	1 g	Saturated	0 g
Sodium	20 mg	Cholesterol	0 mg

· · · · · · · · · · · · · · · ·

Salsa Verde

Tomatillos are the basis of Mexican and Southwestern green sauces and salsas. Look for bright green tomatillos with their husks drawn tightly around them. After husking, rinse well to remove the sticky residue.

¼ cup chopped onion (about 1 small)
2 tablespoons lightly packed cilantro
2 tablespoons lightly packed watercress
1 teaspoon vegetable oil
¼ teaspoon salt
8 ounces tomatillos, cut in half
1 to 2 small green chilies, seeded

Place all ingredients in blender or food processor. Cover and blend or process until smooth. Cover and refrigerate any remaining salsa.

About 1 cup salsa

	Per Tablespoon		
Calories	10	Fat	0 g
Protein	0 g	Unsaturated	0 g
Carbohydrate	1 g	Saturated	0 g
Sodium	35 mg	Cholesterol	0 mg

· · · · · · · · · · · · · · · ·

Lemony Cocktail Sauce

Ground lemon, rind and all, makes the sauce unusually good with cooked shrimp, oysters, clams and mussels.

½ lemon, cut into fourths and seeded
¾ cup chili sauce
1 teaspoon prepared horseradish
1 clove garlic, crushed

Place lemon in blender or food processor. Cover and blend or process until finely ground. Mix lemon and remaining ingredients in glass or plastic bowl. Cover tightly and refrigerate about 1 hour or until chilled.

About 1 cup sauce

	Per Tablespoon		
Calories	10	Fat	0 g
Protein	0 g	Unsaturated	0 g
Carbohydrate	3 g	Saturated	0 g
Sodium	150 mg	Cholesterol	0 mg

Lemony Cocktail Sauce

Pineapple Salsa

½ cup finely chopped red bell pepper (about 1 small)
¼ cup finely chopped red onion (about 1 small)
1 small red chili, seeded and finely chopped
2 cups ½-inch pieces pineapple (about ½ medium)
2 tablespoons chopped cilantro
2 tablespoons lime juice

Cook bell pepper, onion and chili in 8-inch nonstick skillet over medium heat, stirring frequently, until tender. Stir in remaining ingredients. Cover and refrigerate about 2 hours or until chilled.

About 2½ cups salsa

Per Tablespoon			
Calories	5	Fat	0 g
Protein	0 g	Unsaturated	0 g
Carbohydrate	1 g	Saturated	0 g
Sodium	0 mg	Cholesterol	0 mg

Sweet Pepper Relish

1 medium red bell pepper
1 medium yellow bell pepper
1 medium green bell pepper
2 tablespoons pine nuts, toasted
1 tablespoon chopped fresh or 1 teaspoon dried basil
1 tablespoon red wine vinegar
¼ teaspoon salt
2 cloves garlic, crushed

Set oven control to broil. Place bell peppers on rack in broiler pan. Broil about 5 inches from heat 12 to 16 minutes, turning occasionally, until skin is blistered and evenly browned. Place peppers in plastic bag; close tightly. Let stand 15 to 20 minutes. Peel peppers; remove stems, seeds and membranes.

Chop peppers. Mix peppers and remaining ingredients. Cover and refrigerate at least 1 hour.

About 1¼ cups relish

Per Tablespoon			
Calories	10	Fat	0 g
Protein	0 g	Unsaturated	0 g
Carbohydrate	1 g	Saturated	0 g
Sodium	30 mg	Cholesterol	0 mg

Clockwise, from top: Tropical Mahimahi (page 94), Cucumber-Yogurt Sauce (page 170), Pineapple Salsa, Tartar Sauce (page 169)

Chapter 7
Delicious Desserts

♦ Eat sugary desserts in moderation, but when it comes to fresh fruit you can really go to town. Enjoy it chopped, pureed, cold, hot, with sauces or without. Always use ripe fruit for the most flavorful results.

♦ When recipes call for such products as whipped cream, sour cream, cream cheese and ricotta cheese, use low-fat versions.

♦ Angel food cake is a perfect dessert for the low-fat, low-cholesterol crowd. In the pages that follow, we've shown three ways to dress it up: topped with fruit, stuffed with sherbet and in trifle. You can improvise happily from there.

♦ Meringues are egg-yolk-free, and nearly guilt-free. They are extremely versatile. Lemon Meringue Cake with Strawberries (page 181) uses meringue in place of a fatty frosting. Blueberry-Lime Torte (page 193) is a stunning dessert with meringue rather than cake as a base.

♦ Fresh fruit ices and sherbets can be made easily without any eggs or cream, a boon to fat watchers. Combine luscious complementary fruits for seemingly endless variety.

Blueberry-Lime Torte (page 193)

Fruit-topped Angel Food Cake

Angel food cake, made without fat or even yolks, is the perfect answer to a sweet tooth. It's delicious without any topping at all, and you can leave out the almond flavoring if you like.

¾ cup powdered sugar
½ cup cake flour
¾ cup egg whites (about 6)
¾ teaspoon cream of tartar
½ cup granulated sugar
½ teaspoon vanilla
¼ teaspoon almond extract
⅛ teaspoon salt
Fruit Topping (right)
2 tablespoons flaked coconut, toasted

Heat oven to 350°. Mix powdered sugar and flour; reserve. Beat egg whites and cream of tartar in large bowl on high speed until foamy. Beat in granulated sugar, 2 tablespoons at a time, on high speed, adding vanilla, almond extract and salt with last addition of sugar. Continue beating until stiff and glossy. Do not underbeat.

Sprinkle sugar-flour mixture, ¼ cup at a time, over meringue, folding in just until mixture disappears. Spread batter in ungreased loaf pan, 9 × 5 × 3 inches.

Bake 25 to 35 minutes or until cracks feel dry and top springs back when touched lightly. Snap spring-type wooden clothespins on corners of pan for "legs." Invert pan about 2 hours or until cake is completely cool. (Or invert pan, resting edges of pan on 2 other inverted pans to cool.) Remove from pan. Top each serving with Fruit Topping. Sprinkle with coconut.

8 servings (with about ⅓ cup topping each)

FRUIT TOPPING

½ package (2.8-ounce size) whipped topping mix (1 envelope)
3 tablespoons powdered sugar
½ cup skim milk
¼ teaspoon coconut extract
1 cup cut-up pared mango (about 1 medium)
½ cup cut-up pared kiwifruit (about 1 medium)

Mix topping mix (dry), powdered sugar, milk and coconut extract in small deep bowl. Beat on high speed 2 to 3 minutes or until thick and fluffy. Fold in mango and kiwifruit.

Per Serving			
Calories	190	Fat	2 g
Protein	4 g	Unsaturated	0 g
Carbohydrate	39 g	Saturated	2 g
Sodium	90 mg	Cholesterol	0 mg

Spicy Plum Cake

2 tablespoons margarine, melted

3 tablespoons packed brown sugar

1 cup sliced medium red plums, apricots or nectarines
   (2 to 3)

1¼ cups all-purpose flour

1 cup sugar

¼ cup margarine, softened

¾ cup skim milk

1½ teaspoons baking powder

1 teaspoon ground cinnamon

1 teaspoon vanilla

¼ teaspoon ground ginger

¼ teaspoon salt

⅛ teaspoon ground nutmeg

2 egg whites

½ package (2.8-ounce size) whipped topping mix
   (1 envelope)

Heat oven to 350°. Spray square pan, 9 × 9 × 2 inches, with nonstick cooking spray. Line pan with waxed paper. Spread melted margarine in pan. Sprinkle with brown sugar. Arrange plums in single layer on brown sugar. Beat remaining ingredients except topping mix in large bowl on low speed 30 seconds, scraping bowl constantly. Beat on high speed 3 minutes, scraping bowl occasionally. Pour over plums.

Bake about 40 minutes or until wooden pick inserted in center comes out clean. Immediately invert onto heatproof plate; let pan remain a few minutes. Prepare topping mix as directed on package—except substitute skim milk for the milk. Serve cake warm with whipped topping.

9 servings

Per Serving			
Calories	270	Fat	9 g
Protein	3 g	Unsaturated	6 g
Carbohydrate	44 g	Saturated	3 g
Sodium	250 mg	Cholesterol	0 mg

...Orange Angel
...ke

1½ cups powdered sugar
¾ cup cake flour
¼ cup cocoa
1½ cups egg whites (about 12)
1½ teaspoons cream of tartar
1 cup granulated sugar
¼ teaspoon salt
3 cups orange sherbet, softened

Move oven rack to lowest position. Heat oven to 375°. Sift together powdered sugar, flour and cocoa. Beat egg whites and cream of tartar in large bowl on medium speed until foamy. Beat in granulated sugar, 2 table-spoons at a time, on high speed, adding salt with the last addition of sugar. Continue beating until stiff and glossy. Do not underbeat.

Sprinkle cocoa mixture, ¼ cup at a time, over me-ringue, folding in just until cocoa mixture disappears. Spread batter in ungreased tube pan, 10 × 4 inches. Gently cut through batter with metal spatula.

Bake 30 to 35 minutes or until cracks feel dry and top springs back when touched lightly. Invert pan onto metal funnel or glass bottle about 2 hours or until cake is completely cool. Remove from pan.

Slice off top of cake about 1 inch down; set aside. Cut down into cake 1 inch from outer edge and 1 inch from edge of hole, leaving substantial "walls" on each side. Remove cake within cuts with curved knife or spoon, being careful to leave a base of cake 1 inch thick. Spoon sherbet into cake cavity; smooth top. Replace top of cake. Cover and freeze about 3 hours or until firm. Serve with Chocolate Sauce (page 199) if desired.

16 servings

Per Serving			
Calories	175	Fat	1 g
Protein	3 g	Unsaturated	0 g
Carbohydrate	39 g	Saturated	1 g
Sodium	85 mg	Cholesterol	5 mg

Chocolate-Orange Angel Food Cake

Lemon Meringue Cake with Strawberries

A meringue frosting makes this cake special. Egg product can't be used to make the meringue, as the fat will keep the egg whites from increasing in volume when beaten.

2 cups sliced strawberries
¼ cup sugar
1¼ cups all-purpose flour
1 cup sugar
¼ cup margarine, softened
½ cup skim milk
1½ teaspoons baking powder
1½ teaspoons grated lemon peel
1 teaspoon vanilla
¼ teaspoon salt
2 egg whites or ¼ cup cholesterol-free egg product
2 egg whites
½ cup sugar

Mix strawberries and ¼ cup sugar. Cover and refrigerate until serving time.

Heat oven to 350°. Spray square pan, 9 × 9 × 2 inches, with nonstick cooking spray. Beat flour, 1 cup sugar, the margarine, milk, baking powder, lemon peel, vanilla, salt and 2 egg whites in large bowl on low speed 30 seconds, scraping bowl constantly. Beat on high speed 2 minutes, scraping bowl occasionally. Pour into pan. Bake 25 to 30 minutes or until wooden pick inserted in center comes out clean.

Increase oven temperature to 400°. Beat 2 egg whites in medium bowl until foamy. Beat in ½ cup sugar, 1 tablespoon at a time. Continue beating until stiff and glossy. Spread over cake. Bake 8 to 10 minutes or until meringue is light brown; cool completely. Top each serving with strawberries.

9 servings

Per Serving			
Calories	250	Fat	5 g
Protein	4 g	Unsaturated	4 g
Carbohydrate	47 g	Saturated	1 g
Sodium	220 mg	Cholesterol	0 mg

Lemon Meringue Cake with Strawberries

Double Chocolate-Date Cake

Chocolate Chip Topping (right)
1 cup hot water
⅔ cup chopped dates
1⅔ cups all-purpose flour
1 cup packed brown sugar
¼ cup cocoa
1 teaspoon baking soda
¼ teaspoon salt
¼ cup vegetable oil
1 teaspoon cider vinegar
½ teaspoon vanilla

Heat oven to 350°. Prepare Chocolate Chip Topping; reserve. Pour hot water over dates in small bowl. Let stand 5 minutes. Drain dates, reserving water. Mix flour, brown sugar, cocoa, baking soda and salt in ungreased square pan, 8 × 8 × 2 inches. Stir in dates. Add enough water to date water to measure 1 cup. Stir water mixture and remaining ingredients into flour mixture. Sprinkle with topping. Bake 35 to 40 minutes or until wooden pick inserted in center comes out clean.

8 servings

CHOCOLATE CHIP TOPPING

2 tablespoons miniature semisweet chocolate chips
2 tablespoons chopped walnuts
2 tablespoons packed brown sugar

Mix all ingredients.

MICROWAVE DIRECTIONS: Prepare as directed—except use round microwavable dish, 8 × 1½ inches. Elevate dish on inverted pie plate in microwave oven. Microwave uncovered on medium (50%) 15 to 17 minutes, rotating dish ¼ turn every 5 minutes, until top springs back when touched lightly. (Center of top may appear moist but will continue to cook while standing.) Let stand uncovered on heatproof surface 10 minutes (do not use rack).

Per Serving			
Calories	460	Fat	8 g
Protein	8 g	Unsaturated	7 g
Carbohydrate	90 g	Saturated	1 g
Sodium	220 mg	Cholesterol	0 mg

Strawberry Margarita Pie

Graham Cracker Shell (right)
2 envelopes unflavored gelatin
½ cup water
3 cups strawberries
⅓ cup sugar
¼ cup tequila
1 tablespoon orange-flavored liqueur
½ package (2.8-ounce size) whipped topping mix
*   (1 envelope)*

Prepare Graham Cracker Shell. Sprinkle gelatin on water in 2-quart saucepan. Let stand 1 minute to soften. Place strawberries, sugar, tequila and liqueur in blender or food processor. Cover and blend or process until smooth. Stir 1 cup strawberry mixture into gelatin mixture in saucepan. Heat over low heat 3 to 5 minutes, stirring constantly, until gelatin is dissolved. Stir in remaining strawberry mixture. Place pan in bowl of ice and water, or refrigerate 30 to 40 minutes, stirring occasionally, just until mixture mounds slightly when dropped from spoon.

Prepare topping mix in large bowl as directed on package—except omit vanilla and substitute skim milk for the milk. Fold strawberry mixture into whipped topping. Spoon into pie shell. Sprinkle with reserved crumb mixture from shell. Refrigerate about 2 hours or until set.

8 servings

GRAHAM CRACKER SHELL

1¼ cups graham cracker crumbs
2 tablespoons strawberry jelly
1 tablespoon vegetable oil

Spray pie plate, 9 × 1¼ inches, with nonstick cooking spray. Mix all ingredients. Reserve 2 tablespoons mixture for topping. Press remaining mixture firmly against bottom and side of pie plate.

Per Serving			
Calories	180	Fat	5 g
Protein	3 g	Unsaturated	3 g
Carbohydrate	30 g	Saturated	2 g
Sodium	115 mg	Cholesterol	0 mg

Strawberry Margarita Pie

Tropical Fruit Cream Pie

Cookie Shell (below)
⅔ cup sugar
¼ cup cornstarch
½ teaspoon salt
2½ cups skim milk
3 egg whites or ½ cup cholesterol-free egg product
2 tablespoons margarine
1½ teaspoons coconut extract
½ teaspoon vanilla
1½ cups sliced papaya, strawberries and kiwifruit

Bake Cookie Shell; cool completely. Mix sugar, cornstarch and salt in 2-quart saucepan. Gradually stir in milk. Cook over medium heat, stirring constantly, until mixture thickens and boils. Boil and stir 1 minute. Gradually stir half of the hot mixture into egg whites. Stir into remaining hot mixture in saucepan. Boil and stir 1 minute; remove from heat. Stir in margarine, coconut extract and vanilla. Pour into pie shell. Press plastic wrap or waxed paper onto filling. Refrigerate at least 6 hours. Arrange fruit on pie just before serving.

8 servings

COOKIE SHELL

1½ cups gingersnap cookie crumbs (about 25 two-inch cookies)
1 tablespoon margarine, melted
1 egg white or 2 tablespoons cholesterol-free egg product

Heat oven to 350°. Spray pie plate, 9 × 1¼ inches, with nonstick cooking spray. Mix all ingredients. Press firmly against bottom and side of pie plate with fingers dipped in flour. Bake about 10 minutes or until set.

Per Serving			
Calories	255	Fat	9 g
Protein	5 g	Unsaturated	5 g
Carbohydrate	38 g	Saturated	4 g
Sodium	360 mg	Cholesterol	10 mg

Bourbon-Oatmeal Pie

Pastry (below)
1 cup sugar
1 cup dark corn syrup
¼ cup margarine, melted
2 tablespoons bourbon
1 teaspoon vanilla
1 whole egg plus 3 egg whites
1 cup regular oats

Heat oven to 350°. Prepare Pastry. Beat remaining ingredients except oats. Stir in oats. Pour oatmeal mixture into pastry-lined pie plate. Bake 45 to 50 minutes or until center is set.

8 servings

PASTRY

1⅓ cups all-purpose flour
¼ teaspoon salt
½ cup firm margarine
4 to 5 tablespoons cold water

Mix flour and salt. Cut in margarine with pastry blender until particles are size of small peas. Sprinkle in water, 1 tablespoon at a time, tossing with fork until all flour is moistened and pastry almost cleans side of bowl. Gather pastry into a ball. Shape into flattened round on lightly floured cloth-covered surface.

Roll pastry 2 inches larger than inverted pie plate, 9 × 1¼ inches, with floured cloth-covered rolling pin. Fold pastry into fourths; place in plate with point in center. Unfold and ease into plate. Trim overhanging edge of pastry 1 inch from rim of plate. Fold and roll pastry under, even with plate; flute.

Per Serving			
Calories	460	Fat	18 g
Protein	4 g	Unsaturated	15 g
Carbohydrate	70 g	Saturated	3 g
Sodium	340 mg	Cholesterol	25 mg

Bourbon-Oatmeal Pie, top, Easy Pumpkin-Orange Pie (page 188), bottom

Easy Pumpkin-Orange Pie

This custardy pumpkin pie doesn't need a crust.

> *Brown Sugar Topping (below)*
> *1 can (16 ounces) pumpkin*
> *1 can (12 ounces) evaporated skimmed milk*
> *3 egg whites or ½ cup cholesterol-free egg product*
> *½ cup sugar*
> *½ cup all-purpose flour*
> *1½ teaspoons pumpkin pie spice*
> *¾ teaspoon baking powder*
> *⅛ teaspoon salt*
> *2 teaspoons grated orange peel*

Heat oven to 350°. Prepare Brown Sugar Topping. Spray pie plate, 10 × 1½ inches, with nonstick cooking spray. Place remaining ingredients in blender or food processor in order listed. Cover and blend or process until smooth. Pour into pie plate. Sprinkle with topping. Bake 50 to 55 minutes or until knife inserted in center comes out clean. Cool 15 minutes. Refrigerate about 4 hours or until chilled.

8 servings

BROWN SUGAR TOPPING

> *¼ cup packed brown sugar*
> *¼ cup quick-cooking oats*
> *1 tablespoon margarine, softened*

Mix all ingredients.

MICROWAVE DIRECTIONS: Prepare as directed—except use microwavable pie plate. Elevate pie plate on inverted microwavable dinner plate in microwave oven. Microwave uncovered on medium (50%) 20 to 30 minutes, rotating pie plate ¼ turn every 5 minutes, until center is set. Let stand uncovered 15 minutes on flat, heatproof surface.

Per Serving			
Calories	175	Fat	2 g
Protein	6 g	Unsaturated	1 g
Carbohydrate	35 g	Saturated	<1 g
Sodium	175 mg	Cholesterol	0 mg

Rice Pudding

A light sifting of cinnamon enhances the top of the microwaved version.

> *2 egg whites*
> *1 egg*
> *2 cups cooked rice*
> *½ cup sugar*
> *½ cup golden raisins*
> *2 cups skim milk*
> *½ teaspoon vanilla*
> *¼ teaspoon ground cardamom*

Heat oven to 325°. Beat egg whites and egg in ungreased 1½-quart casserole. Stir in remaining ingredients. Bake uncovered 50 to 60 minutes, stirring after 30 minutes, until knife inserted halfway between center and edge comes out clean. Serve warm or cold. Immediately refrigerate any remaining pudding.

8 servings (about ½ cup each)

MICROWAVE DIRECTIONS: Prepare as directed—except use 1½-quart microwavable casserole and decrease skim milk to 1½ cups. Elevate casserole on inverted microwavable pie plate in microwave oven. Microwave uncovered on medium (50%) 8 to 10 minutes, stirring every 3 minutes, just until creamy. (Pudding will continue to cook while standing.) Let stand uncovered on heatproof surface 10 minutes. Sprinkle with ground cinnamon if desired. Cover and refrigerate any remaining pudding.

Per Serving			
Calories	170	Fat	1 g
Protein	5 g	Unsaturated	1 g
Carbohydrate	36 g	Saturated	0 g
Sodium	245 mg	Cholesterol	30 mg

Pineapple Bread Pudding with Rum Sauce

4 egg whites
½ teaspoon cream of tartar
½ cup sugar
½ teaspoon ground cinnamon
¼ cup margarine, melted
1 can (8 ounces) crushed pineapple in juice, well drained and juice reserved
2 cups ½-inch soft bread cubes (about 3 slices bread)
2 tablespoons chopped pecans
Rum Sauce (right)

Heat oven to 325°. Spray round baking dish, 8 × 1½ × 1 inches, with nonstick cooking spray. Beat egg whites and cream of tartar in large bowl until foamy. Beat in sugar, 1 tablespoon at a time. Continue beating until stiff and glossy. Do not underbeat. Beat in cinnamon.

Fold margarine, pineapple and bread cubes into meringue. Pour into casserole. Sprinkle with pecans. Bake uncovered 30 to 35 minutes or until knife inserted in center comes out clean. Serve with Rum Sauce. Cover and refrigerate any remaining pudding.

6 servings (about ¾ cup each)

RUM SAUCE

3 tablespoons sugar
1 tablespoon cornstarch
Reserved pineapple juice
1 tablespoon rum

Mix sugar and cornstarch in 1-quart saucepan. Add water to pineapple juice to measure 1 cup. Gradually stir into sugar mixture. Cook over medium heat, stirring constantly, until mixture thickens and boils. Boil and stir 1 minute; remove from heat. Stir in rum. Serve warm over bread pudding.

Per Serving			
Calories	250	Fat	10 g
Protein	3 g	Unsaturated	8 g
Carbohydrate	37 g	Saturated	2 g
Sodium	175 mg	Cholesterol	0 mg

Apple Custard with Caramel Sauce

2 medium cooking apples, pared, cored and cut in half
½ cup sugar
½ teaspoon vanilla
5 egg whites or ¾ cup cholesterol-free egg product*
2 drops yellow food color
Dash of salt
1½ cups skim milk, scalded
Ground cinnamon
Caramel Sauce (below)

Heat oven to 350°. Spray four 10-ounce custard cups with nonstick cooking spray. Place apple half, cut side down, in each cup. Beat sugar, vanilla, egg whites, food color and salt. Gradually stir in milk. Pour over apples. Sprinkle with cinnamon. Place cups in rectangular pan, 13 × 9 × 2 inches, on oven rack. Pour very hot water into pan to within ½ inch of tops of cups.

Bake 40 to 50 minutes or until knife inserted in custard comes out clean. Remove cups from water. Refrigerate until chilled. Serve with Caramel Sauce.

4 servings (with about 2½ tablespoons sauce each)

▪ CARAMEL SAUCE

⅓ cup packed brown sugar
¼ cup light corn syrup
2 tablespoons water
1 tablespoon margarine
½ teaspoon vanilla

Mix all ingredients except vanilla in saucepan. Cook over medium heat, stirring constantly, just until sugar is dissolved; remove from heat. Stir in vanilla. Serve warm or cold. Stir thoroughly before serving.

*If using cholesterol-free egg product, omit food color.

Per Serving			
Calories	345	Fat	3 g
Protein	7 g	Unsaturated	2 g
Carbohydrate	73 g	Saturated	1 g
Sodium	240 mg	Cholesterol	2 mg

· · · · · · · · · · · · · · · · · ·

Individual Cranberry-Orange Desserts

3 egg whites
1 egg yolk
½ cup skim milk
2 teaspoons grated orange peel
¼ cup orange juice
1 cup sugar
⅓ cup all-purpose flour
¼ teaspoon salt
¾ cup cranberry halves

Heat oven to 350°. Beat egg whites in large bowl on high speed until stiff peaks form. Beat egg yolk slightly in medium bowl on medium speed. Beat in milk, orange peel and orange juice. Beat in sugar, flour and salt until smooth. Stir in cranberry halves.

Fold egg yolk mixture into egg whites. Divide among 4 ungreased 10-ounce ramekins or custard cups. Place ramekins in rectangular pan, 13 × 9 × 2 inches, on oven rack. Pour very hot water (1 inch deep) into pan. Bake about 30 minutes or until golden brown. Serve warm or cold. Sprinkle lightly with powdered sugar if desired.

4 servings

Per Serving			
Calories	275	Fat	2 g
Protein	5 g	Unsaturated	2 g
Carbohydrate	62 g	Saturated	0 g
Sodium	200 mg	Cholesterol	55 mg

Individual Cranberry-Orange Desserts

Lemon-Ginger Trifle with Apricots

Homemade, store-bought and made-from-a-mix angel food cakes all work well in this recipe. A 7-inch loaf yields about 6 cups of cake cubes; a 7½-inch ring yields about 11 cups.

¾ cup sugar
2 tablespoons cornstarch
¼ teaspoon salt
1¼ cups water
1 teaspoon grated lemon peel
¼ cup lemon juice
2 teaspoons margarine
1½ teaspoons grated gingerroot or ½ teaspoon
  ground ginger
½ package (2.8-ounce size) whipped topping mix
  (1 envelope)
8 cups 1-inch cubes angel food cake
6 large apricots, thinly sliced*

Mix sugar, cornstarch and salt in 2-quart saucepan. Gradually stir in water. Cook over medium heat, stirring constantly, until mixture thickens and boils. Boil and stir 1 minute; remove from heat. Stir in lemon peel, lemon juice, margarine and gingerroot. Press plastic wrap or waxed paper onto surface. Refrigerate about 4 hours or until chilled.

Prepare whipped topping mix as directed on package—except use skim milk. Reserve ¾ cup whipped topping. Fold lemon mixture into remaining whipped topping.

Place ⅓ of the cake cubes in large clear glass bowl. Spread ⅓ of the lemon mixture over cake cubes. Top with ⅓ of the apricots. Repeat twice. Spread reserved whipped topping over top. Garnish with lemon curls if desired. Cover and refrigerate up to 8 hours.

8 servings (about 1 cup each)

MICROWAVE DIRECTIONS: Decrease water to 1 cup. Mix sugar, cornstarch and salt in 4-cup microwavable measure. Gradually stir in water. Microwave uncovered on high 3 to 4 minutes, stirring every minute, until boiling. Continue as directed.

*1 can (16 ounces) apricots in juice, well drained and sliced, can be substituted for the fresh apricots.

Per Serving			
Calories	335	Fat	3 g
Protein	5 g	Unsaturated	1 g
Carbohydrate	73 g	Saturated	2 g
Sodium	200 mg	Cholesterol	0 mg

Blueberry-Lime Torte

Fresh blueberries and lime cream are mounded in a crisp, meringue shell.

Meringue Shell (right)
2 egg whites
1 egg
½ cup sugar
⅔ cup water
⅓ cup lime juice
1 envelope unflavored gelatin
1 tablespoon grated lime peel
4 egg whites
½ teaspoon cream of tartar
½ cup sugar
1½ cups blueberries

Bake Meringue Shell; cool completely. Beat 2 egg whites and the egg in medium bowl until foamy. Mix ½ cup sugar, the water, lime juice and gelatin in 2-quart nonstick saucepan. Heat to boiling over medium heat, stirring constantly. Gradually stir at least half of the hot mixture into egg mixture. Stir into hot mixture in saucepan. Heat to boiling; remove from heat. Stir in lime peel. Place pan in bowl of ice and water, or refrigerate about 15 minutes, stirring occasionally, until mixture mounds when dropped from spoon.

Beat 4 egg whites and the cream of tartar in large bowl until foamy. Beat in ½ cup sugar, 1 tablespoon at a time. Continue beating until stiff and glossy. Do not underbeat. Fold in lime mixture. Place blueberries in shell. Spoon lime mixture over blueberries. Refrigerate about 3 hours or until set. Garnish with lime twist and blueberries if desired.

8 servings

MERINGUE SHELL

3 egg whites
¼ teaspoon cream of tartar
¾ cup sugar

Heat oven to 275°. Line cookie sheet with cooking parchment paper or aluminum foil. Beat egg whites and cream of tartar in medium bowl until foamy. Beat in sugar, 1 tablespoon at a time. Continue beating until stiff and glossy. Do not underbeat. Shape meringue on cookie sheet into 9-inch circle with back of spoon, building up side. Bake 1 hour. Turn off oven. Leave meringue in oven with door closed 1½ hours. Finish cooling meringue at room temperature.

Per Serving			
Calories	210	Fat	1 g
Protein	5 g	Unsaturated	0 g
Carbohydrate	47 g	Saturated	<1 g
Sodium	70 mg	Cholesterol	25 mg

·late Swirl Cheesecake with Raspberry Topping

4 chocolate wafers, crushed (about ¼ cup)
2 cups Thick Yogurt (page 35)
1 package (8 ounces) Neufchâtel cheese, softened
⅔ cup sugar
¼ cup skim milk
2 tablespoons all-purpose flour
2 teaspoons vanilla
3 egg whites or ½ cup cholesterol-free egg product
1 tablespoon cocoa
1 teaspoon chocolate extract
Raspberry Topping (right)

Heat oven to 300°. Spray springform pan, 9 × 3 inches, with nonstick cooking spray. Sprinkle chocolate wafer crumbs on bottom of pan. Beat Thick Yogurt and cheese in medium bowl on medium speed until smooth. Add sugar, milk, flour, vanilla and egg whites. Beat on medium speed about 2 minutes or until smooth.

Place 1 cup batter in small bowl. Beat in cocoa and chocolate extract until blended. Carefully spread vanilla batter over crumbs in pan. Drop chocolate batter by spoonfuls onto vanilla batter. Swirl through batter with metal spatula for marbled effect, being careful not to touch bottom.

Bake 1 hour. Turn off oven; leave cheesecake in oven 30 minutes. Remove from oven; cool 15 minutes. Prepare Raspberry Topping; spread over cheesecake. Cover and refrigerate at least 3 hours. Or, spoon Raspberry Topping over individual servings of chilled cheesecake.

12 servings (with about 2 tablespoons topping each)

RASPBERRY TOPPING

1 package (10 ounces) frozen raspberries, thawed, drained and juice reserved
¼ cup sugar
2 tablespoons cornstarch

Add enough water to reserved juice to measure 1¼ cups. Mix sugar and cornstarch in 1½-quart saucepan. Stir in juice mixture and raspberries. Heat to boiling over medium heat, stirring frequently. Boil and stir 1 minute; cool.

Per Serving			
Calories	195	Fat	5 g
Protein	6 g	Unsaturated	2 g
Carbohydrate	32 g	Saturated	3 g
Sodium	150 mg	Cholesterol	15 mg

Chocolate Swirl Cheesecake with Raspberry Topping
Following Pages: Blackberry-Peach Crisp (page 198), left, Pineapple Bread Pudding with Rum Sauce (page 189), right

Blackberry-Peach Crisp

There's something warm and cozy about an old-fashioned fruit crisp. Nectarines can replace the peaches; for tarter flavor, try fresh apricots.

2 cups blackberries*
1 tablespoon cornstarch
3 cups sliced peaches or nectarines (about 3 medium)
¾ cup packed brown sugar
½ cup whole wheat flour
½ cup regular oats
¼ cup margarine
¾ teaspoon ground cinnamon
½ teaspoon ground nutmeg

Heat oven to 375°. Place blackberries in large bowl. Sprinkle with cornstarch. Toss until blackberries are coated. Carefully stir in peaches. Place fruit in ungreased square baking dish, 8 × 8 × 2 inches. Mix remaining ingredients. Sprinkle over fruit. Bake about 30 minutes or until topping is golden brown and fruit is tender.

8 servings

*1 package (16 ounces) frozen blackberries, thawed, and 1 package (16 ounces) frozen sliced peaches, thawed, can be substituted for the fresh blackberries and peaches.

Per Serving			
Calories	200	Fat	6 g
Protein	2 g	Unsaturated	5 g
Carbohydrate	37 g	Saturated	1 g
Sodium	95 mg	Cholesterol	0 mg

Creamy Peach Freeze

½ cup cholesterol-free egg product
⅔ cup sugar
1½ cups skim milk
¼ teaspoon salt
2 cups mashed peeled peaches (4 to 5 medium)*
2 teaspoons vanilla
2 containers (8 ounces each) peach nonfat yogurt

Mix egg product, sugar, milk and salt in 2-quart saucepan. Cook over medium heat, stirring constantly, just until bubbles appear around edge. Pour into chilled large metal bowl. Refrigerate 1½ to 2 hours, stirring occasionally, until room temperature.

Stir peaches, vanilla and yogurt into milk mixture. Freeze as directed by manufacturer of ice-cream maker.

8 servings (about ½ cup each)

MICROWAVE DIRECTIONS: Place milk in 4-cup microwavable measure. Microwave uncovered on high 2 to 3 minutes or until very warm. Beat in egg product, sugar and salt. Microwave uncovered on medium-high (70%) 3 to 4 minutes, stirring every minute, until thickened. Continue as directed.

*1 package (16 ounces) frozen sliced peaches, thawed and mashed, can be substituted for the fresh peaches.

Per Serving			
Calories	130	Fat	0 g
Protein	6 g	Unsaturated	0 g
Carbohydrate	26 g	Saturated	0 g
Sodium	150 mg	Cholesterol	0 mg

Chocolate Sauce

½ cup sugar
¼ cup cocoa
1 tablespoon cornstarch
1 can (12 ounces) evaporated skimmed milk
1 teaspoon vanilla

Mix sugar, cocoa and cornstarch in 1½-quart saucepan. Gradually stir in milk. Heat over medium heat, stirring constantly, until mixture thickens and boils; remove from heat. Stir in vanilla. (Beat with wire whisk if sauce becomes lumpy.) Serve warm, or press plastic wrap or waxed paper onto surface and refrigerate until chilled.

About 1¾ cups sauce

MICROWAVE DIRECTIONS: Mix sugar, cocoa and cornstarch in 4-cup microwavable measure. Gradually stir in milk. Microwave uncovered on high 3 to 5 minutes, stirring every minute, until boiling. Stir in vanilla.

Per Tablespoon			
Calories	35	Fat	0 g
Protein	1 g	Unsaturated	0 g
Carbohydrate	7 g	Saturated	0 g
Sodium	15 mg	Cholesterol	0 mg

Peppermint Brownies

1 cup sugar
⅓ cup margarine, softened
1 teaspoon vanilla
½ teaspoon peppermint extract
3 egg whites or ½ cup cholesterol-free egg product
⅔ cup all-purpose flour
½ cup cocoa
½ teaspoon baking powder
¼ teaspoon salt
Chocolate Glaze (below)
2 tablespoons crushed peppermint candy

Heat oven to 350°. Spray square pan, 8 × 8 × 2 inches, with nonstick cooking spray. Mix sugar, margarine, vanilla, peppermint extract and egg whites in medium bowl. Stir in remaining ingredients except Chocolate Glaze and candy. Spread in pan.

Bake 20 to 25 minutes or until wooden pick inserted in center comes out clean; cool. Spread Chocolate Glaze evenly over brownies. Sprinkle with candy. Cut into about 2-inch squares.

16 brownies

CHOCOLATE GLAZE

⅔ cup powdered sugar
2 tablespoons cocoa
3 to 4 teaspoons hot water
¼ teaspoon vanilla

Mix all ingredients until smooth and desired consistency.

Per Brownie			
Calories	125	Fat	4 g
Protein	1 g	Unsaturated	3 g
Carbohydrate	22 g	Saturated	1 g
Sodium	95 mg	Cholesterol	0 mg

Apricot-Meringue Squares

Any flavor of jam is delicious in this recipe. To make cutting the dessert into squares easier, simply wet the knife to keep it from sticking.

1 cup all-purpose flour
¼ cup powdered sugar
¼ cup margarine, softened
1 egg white
2 egg whites
½ cup granulated sugar
½ cup apricot jam
3 tablespoons miniature semisweet chocolate chips

Heat oven to 350°. Spray square pan, 9 × 9 × 2 inches, with nonstick cooking spray. Mix flour, powdered sugar, margarine and 1 egg white. Press in pan. Bake about 15 minutes or until set.

Increase oven temperature to 400°. Beat 2 egg whites until foamy. Beat in granulated sugar, 1 tablespoon at a time. Continue beating until stiff and glossy. Spread jam over baked layer. Sprinkle with chocolate chips. Spread meringue over jam and chocolate chips. Bake about 10 minutes or until meringue is brown. Cool completely. Cut into 1½-inch squares.

25 squares

Per Square			
Calories	80	Fat	2 g
Protein	1 g	Unsaturated	1 g
Carbohydrate	14 g	Saturated	1 g
Sodium	30 mg	Cholesterol	0 mg

Frosted Banana Bars

⅔ cup sugar
½ cup lowfat sour cream
2 tablespoons margarine, softened
2 egg whites or ¼ cup cholesterol-free egg product
¾ cup mashed very ripe bananas (about 2 medium)
1 teaspoon vanilla
1 cup all-purpose flour
¼ teaspoon salt
½ teaspoon baking soda
2 tablespoons finely chopped walnuts
Frosting (below)

Heat oven to 375°. Spray square pan, 9 × 9 × 2 inches, with nonstick cooking spray. Beat sugar, sour cream, margarine and egg whites in large bowl on low speed 1 minute, scraping bowl occasionally. Beat in bananas and vanilla on low speed 30 seconds. Beat in flour, salt and baking soda on medium speed 1 minute, scraping bowl occasionally. Stir in nuts. Spread in pan.

Bake 20 to 25 minutes or until light brown; cool. Spread with Frosting. Cut into 2¼ × 1½-inch bars.

24 bars

FROSTING

1¼ cups powdered sugar
1 tablespoon margarine, softened
1 to 2 tablespoons skim milk
½ teaspoon vanilla

Mix all ingredients until smooth.

Per Bar			
Calories	90	Fat	2 g
Protein	1 g	Unsaturated	1 g
Carbohydrate	18 g	Saturated	<1 g
Sodium	70 mg	Cholesterol	2 mg

Apricot-Meringue Squares, Frosted Banana Bars

Chocolate Chip Cookies

This cookie uses half the fat and half the chips of ordinary recipes, but you won't miss them. Miniature chocolate chips give the illusion of more chocolate because they distribute so well.

½ cup granulated sugar
¼ cup packed brown sugar
¼ cup margarine, softened
1 teaspoon vanilla
1 egg white or 2 tablespoons cholesterol-free egg product
1 cup all-purpose flour
½ teaspoon baking soda
¼ teaspoon salt
½ cup miniature semisweet chocolate chips

Heat oven to 375°. Mix sugars, margarine, vanilla and egg white in large bowl. Stir in flour, baking soda and salt. Stir in chocolate chips. Drop dough by rounded teaspoonfuls about 2 inches apart onto ungreased cookie sheet. Bake 8 to 10 minutes or until golden brown. Cool slightly; remove from cookie sheet.

About 2½ dozen cookies

Per Cookie			
Calories	75	Fat	2 g
Protein	1 g	Unsaturated	2 g
Carbohydrate	14 g	Saturated	0 g
Sodium	65 mg	Cholesterol	0 mg

Cocoa-Oatmeal Cookies

The dough may seem too liquid at first, but the oats and cocoa will absorb the excess moisture. Carob chips may be substituted in this recipe. They have a sweet, distinctive flavor. To make them "go farther," you can chop them up a bit.

1½ cups sugar
½ cup margarine, softened
½ cup plain nonfat yogurt
¼ cup water
1 teaspoon vanilla
½ teaspoon chocolate extract, if desired
2 egg whites or ¼ cup cholesterol-free egg product
3 cups quick-cooking oats
1¼ cups all-purpose flour
½ cup miniature semisweet chocolate chips*
⅓ cup cocoa
½ teaspoon baking soda
¼ teaspoon salt

Heat oven to 350°. Mix sugar, margarine, yogurt, water, vanilla, chocolate extract and egg whites in large bowl. Stir in remaining ingredients. Drop dough by rounded teaspoonfuls about 2 inches apart onto ungreased cookie sheet. Bake 9 to 11 minutes or until almost no indentation remains when touched.

About 5½ dozen cookies

*½ cup carob chips can be substituted for the chocolate chips.

Per Cookie			
Calories	45	Fat	2 g
Protein	1 g	Unsaturated	2 g
Carbohydrate	7 g	Saturated	0 g
Sodium	50 mg	Cholesterol	0 mg

Chocolate Chip Cookies, Cocoa-Oatmeal Cookies

Capped Fig Cookies

Fig Filling (right)
1 cup packed brown sugar
⅓ cup margarine, softened
¼ cup buttermilk
2 egg whites
1¾ cups all-purpose flour
1 teaspoon vanilla
½ teaspoon baking soda
½ teaspoon salt
⅛ teaspoon ground cinnamon

Heat oven to 400°. Prepare Fig Filling. Mix brown sugar, margarine, buttermilk and egg whites in large bowl. Stir in remaining ingredients. Drop dough by teaspoonfuls about 2 inches apart onto ungreased cookie sheet. Top each with ½ teaspoon filling. Top filling with ½ teaspoon dough. Bake 8 to 10 minutes or until almost no indentation remains when touched (do not touch filling). Immediately remove from cookie sheet; cool. Store tightly covered.

About 3 dozen cookies

FIG FILLING

1 cup finely chopped dried figs (about 8)
⅓ cup sugar
¼ cup water
1 tablespoon lemon juice
3 tablespoons chopped walnuts

Heat figs, sugar, water and lemon juice in 1-quart saucepan over medium heat, stirring constantly, until mixture thickens and boils. Stir in walnuts; cool.

Per Cookie			
Calories	80	Fat	2 g
Protein	1 g	Unsaturated	2 g
Carbohydrate	15 g	Saturated	0 g
Sodium	75 mg	Cholesterol	0 mg

Capped Fig Cookies, Creamy Peach Freeze (page 198)

Italian Biscotti

1 cup sugar
½ cup margarine
5 egg whites or ¾ cup cholesterol-free egg product
1¼ teaspoons almond extract
3½ cups all-purpose flour
1 teaspoon baking powder
½ teaspoon salt
2 cups ground toasted almonds (8 ounces)

Heat oven to 350°. Grease rectangular pan, 13 × 9 × 2 inches. Beat sugar and margarine in large bowl until creamy. Beat in egg whites and almond extract on high speed about 2 minutes or until light and fluffy. Stir in flour, baking powder and salt. Stir in almonds. Spread in pan. Bake 25 to 30 minutes or until wooden pick inserted in center comes out clean. Cool completely.

Heat oven to 350° Cut cake crosswise into four 3-inch strips. Cut strips crosswise into ½-inch slices. Place on ungreased cookie sheet. Bake 20 to 25 minutes or until crisp and brown.

About 4 dozen biscotti

Per Cookie			
Calories	95	Fat	4 g
Protein	2 g	Unsaturated	3 g
Carbohydrate	11 g	Saturated	<1 g
Sodium	60 mg	Cholesterol	0 mg

Italian Biscotti

APPENDICES

Reading a Nutrition Label

The amount of fat includes saturated, polyunsaturated and monounsaturated fat. Although it's not required, some labels also break out the amounts of unsaturated and saturated fatty acids.

Cholesterol amounts listed on the label are optional unless there is a product claim about cholesterol on the package. Many manufacturers voluntarily list the cholesterol content of a product.

To determine the percentage of calories in the product from fat, multiply the grams of fat by 9 (1 gram of fat equals 9 calories). Then divide that number by the total number of calories per serving. To get a percent, multiply by 100. The percent of calories coming from fat, here, is 9%. Remember, although experts recommend that the total diet not exceed 30% of calories from fat, not every food must be low in fat.

$$1 \text{ gram of fat} \times \frac{9 \text{ calories}}{1 \text{ gram of fat}} = 9 \text{ calories}$$

$$\frac{9 \text{ calories}}{100 \text{ total calories in 1 serving}} \times 100 = 9\% \text{ of calories from fat}$$

The manufacturer's name and place of business must be included on the label, although it doesn't always appear on the nutrition information panel.

Information about the type of carbohydrate in a product is voluntarily provided by some manufacturers. Divide the number of grams of sucrose by 4 for an estimate of the number of teaspoons of sugar in a serving of the product.

DRY CEREAL
NUTRITION INFORMATION PER SERVING

SERVING SIZE .... 1 OUNCE
SERVINGS PER PACKAGE..................... 12

	1 ounce cereal	cereal plus ½ cup vitamin A & B fortified skim milk†
CALORIES	100	140
PROTEIN, g	3	7
CARBOHYDRATE, g	23	29
FAT, g.....................	1	1
CHOLESTEROL, mg	0	0
SODIUM, mg	200	260
POTASSIUM, mg	110	310

PERCENTAGE OF U.S. RECOMMENDED DAILY ALLOWANCES (U.S. RDA)

PROTEIN	4	10
VITAMIN A	25	30
VITAMIN C	25	25
THIAMIN	25	30
RIBOFLAVIN	25	35
NIACIN	25	25
CALCIUM	4	20
IRON	25	25
VITAMIN D	10	25
VITAMIN B₆	25	30
FOLIC ACID	25	25
PHOSPHORUS	10	20
MAGNESIUM	8	10
ZINC	4	6
COPPER	6	6

INGREDIENTS: WHOLE WHEAT, SUGAR, SALT, CEREAL MALT SYRUP, CALCIUM CARBONATE, CALCIUM CHLORIDE, TRISODIUM PHOSPHATE, VITAMIN C (SODIUM ASCORBATE), A B VITAMIN (NIACINAMIDE), IRON (A MINERAL NUTRIENT), VITAMIN A (PALMITATE), VITAMIN B₆ (PYRIDOXINE HYDROCHLORIDE), VITAMIN B₂ (RIBOFLAVIN), VITAMIN B₁ (THIAMIN MONONITRATE), A B VITAMIN (FOLIC ACID) AND VITAMIN D. FRESHNESS PRESERVED BY BHT

General Mills, Inc.
GENERAL OFFICES MINNEAPOLIS, MINNESOTA 55440
Made in U.S.A.
© 1989 General Mills, Inc.

CARBOHYDRATE INFORMATION

	Cereal 1 ounce	with ½ cup vitamins A & D fortified skim milk†
COMPLEX CARBOHYDRATES, g	17	17
SUCROSE AND OTHER SUGARS, g	3	9
DIETARY FIBER, g	3	3
TOTAL CARBOHYDRATES, g	23	29

VALUES BY FORMULATION
CEREAL PLUS ½ CUP 2% MILK CONTAINS 160 CALORIES, 3 GRAMS OF FAT AND 10 MILLIGRAMS CHOLESTEROL. ALL OTHER NUTRIENTS REMAIN AS LISTED.

The serving size and number of servings in the package are listed. Other nutrition information on the panel relates to the size of a serving.

Some products provide an additional column to show nutrient content when a commonly-added food is also eaten. Cereals often list information about the cereal with ½ cup of skim milk added.

The percent U.S. Recommended Daily Allowances (% U.S. RDA) shows how a product helps meet daily nutrient needs. Information about protein and seven vitamins and minerals must be listed. The manufacturer may list another 12 vitamins and minerals, if specific minimum levels are present in the product. Based on the Recommended Dietary Allowances (RDAs) set by the Food and Nutrition Board of the National Academy of Sciences, the U.S. RDAs are the highest adult RDAs. The RDAs are more specific than the U.S. RDAs, as they provide information about requirements for several age groups of males and females.

The ingredient list must appear on all food products, except those with standards of identity. Ingredients are listed in order of predominance by weight.

Dietary fiber is listed voluntarily, unless a claim about the product's content is made.

A Guide for Heart-Healthy Eating

	CHOOSE MORE . . .	CHOOSE LESS . . .
Meats, Poultry, Fish and Legumes	Lean meats, skinless poultry, fish, shellfish	Fatty meats, organ meats, cold cuts, sausage, hot dogs, bacon
	Split peas, kidney beans, tofu, navy beans, lentils, soybeans	
Milk, Yogurt and Cheese	Skim milk, 1% milk, lowfat buttermilk	Whole milk, 2% milk, cream, half-and-half, whipped toppings, most nondairy creamers
	Lowfat cottage cheese	Whole milk cottage cheese
	Lowfat cheeses, farmer cheese	Hard cheeses, cream cheese, sour cream
	Nonfat or lowfat yogurt	Whole milk yogurt
	Ice milk, sherbet, sorbet	Ice cream
Eggs	Egg whites	Egg yolks
	Cholesterol-free egg substitutes	
Breads and Cereals	Whole-grain breads: whole wheat, pumpernickel, rye; breadsticks, English muffins, bagels, rice cakes, pita bread	Egg bread, croissants, butter rolls
	Oat bran, oatmeal, whole grain cereals	
	Saltines,* zwieback, pretzels,* plain popcorn	Cheese crackers, butter crackers
	Rice, pasta	Egg noodles
	Angel food cake	Sweet rolls, pastries, doughnuts
Fruits and Vegetables	Fresh, frozen or dried fruits and vegetables	Vegetables prepared with butter, cream or cheese sauces
Fats and Oils	Polyunsaturated or mono-unsaturated vegetable oils: sunflower, corn, soybean, olive, safflower, sesame, canola, cottonseed	Saturated fats: coconut oil, palm oil, palm kernel oil, lard, bacon fat
	Margarine or shortening made with polyunsaturated fat	Butter
	Cocoa	Chocolate

*Low-salt varieties

Source: Adapted from *The American Heart Association Diet: An Eating Plan for Healthy Americans*, American Heart Association, Dallas, TX, 1985.

Fat Content of Fish

LEAN FISH
LESS THAN 2.5% FAT

Cod
Haddock
Halibut
Grouper
Mackerel: King
Mahimahi
Ocean Perch
Orange Roughy
Pike
Red Snapper
Sole
Striped Bass
Tuna: Skipjack, Yellowfin

MEDIUM-FAT FISH
2.5–5% FAT

Anchovy
Bluefish
Catfish
Croaker
Mullet
Porgy
Redfish
Salmon: Pink
Shark
Swordfish
Trout: Rainbow, Sea
Tuna: Bluefin
Whitefish

FATTY FISH
MORE THAN 5% FAT

Butterfish
Herring
Mackerel: Atlantic, Pacific, Spanish
Pompano
Sablefish
Salmon: Chinook, Coho, Sockeye
Sardines
Shad
Tuna: Albacore
Trout: Lake

Source: Compiled by General Mills, Inc., from National Fisheries Institute, 1990.

Good Sources of Soluble and Insoluble Fiber

MOSTLY SOLUBLE	CONTAINS BOTH SOLUBLE AND INSOLUBLE	MOSTLY INSOLUBLE
Citrus fruits	Oat bran	Wheat bran
Citrus pectin	Whole-grain oats	Corn bran
Apple pectin	Carrots	Brown rice
	Apples	Cauliflower
	Potatoes	Bananas
	Broccoli	Nuts
		Lentils

Source: Compiled by General Mills, Inc., 1989.

Egg White Substitutions for Whole Eggs*

USE	FOR
2 egg whites	1 whole egg
3 egg whites	2 whole eggs
5 egg whites	3 whole eggs
6 egg whites	4 whole eggs
8 egg whites	5 whole eggs
9 egg whites	6 whole eggs
11 egg whites	7 whole eggs
12 egg whites	8 whole eggs

*Based on whole large eggs (about ¼ cup each).

Source: General Mills, Inc., 1990.

Canadian Metric Conversion Tables

DRY AND LIQUID MEASUREMENTS			TEMPERATURES	
IMPERIAL	**METRIC**		**FAHRENHEIT**	**CELSIUS**
¼ teaspoon	1 mL		32°F	0°C
½ teaspoon	2 mL		212°F	100°C
1 teaspoon	5 mL		250°F	121°C
1 tablespoon	15 mL		275°F	140°C
2 tablespoons	25 mL		300°F	150°C
3 tablespoons	50 mL		325°F	160°C
¼ cup	50 mL		350°F	180°C
⅓ cup	75 mL		375°F	190°C
½ cup	125 mL		400°F	200°C
⅔ cup	150 mL		425°F	220°C
¾ cup	175 mL		450°F	230°C
1 cup	250 mL		475°F	240°C

COMMON COOKING AND BAKING UTENSIL EQUIVALENTS

BAKEWARE	IMPERIAL	METRIC
Round Pan	8 × 1½ inches	20 × 4 cm
	9 × 1½ inches	22 × 4 cm
Square Pan	8 × 8 × 2 inches	22 × 22 × 5 cm
	9 × 9 × 2 inches	23 × 23 × 5 cm
Baking Dishes	11 × 7 × 1½ inches	28 × 18 × 4 cm
	12 × 7½ × 2 inches	30 × 19 × 5 cm
	13 × 9 × 2 inches	33 × 23 × 5 cm
Loaf Pan	8½ × 4½ × 2½ inches	22 × 11 × 6 cm
	9 × 5 × 3 inches	23 × 13 × 8 cm
Tube Pan	10 × 4 inches	25 × 10 cm
Jelly Roll Pan	15½ × 10½ × 1 inch	39 × 27 × 2.5 cm
Pie Plate	9 × 1¼ inches	23 × 3.2 cm
	10 × 1½ inches	25 × 4 cm
Muffin Cups	2½ × 1¼ inches	6 × 3.2 cm
	3 × 1½ inches	8 × 4 cm
Skillet	10 inches	25 cm
Casseroles and	1 quart	1 L
Saucepans	1½ quart	1.5 L
	2 quarts	2 L
	2½ quarts	2.5 L
	3 quarts	3 L
	4 quarts	4 L

NOTE: The recipes in this cookbook have not been developed or tested in Canadian metric measures. When converting to Canadian metric, some variations in recipe quality may be noted.

INDEX

Prentice Hall Press

Vice President and Publisher: Anne M. Zeman
Senior Editor: Rebecca W. Atwater
Assistant Editor: Rachel Simon
Interior Design: Patricia Fabricant
Photography Design: Carmen Bonilla
Prop Stylist: Janice Ervin
Production Editor: Philip Metcalf
Senior Production Manager: Susan Joseph

General Mills, Inc.

Senior Editor: Karen Couné
Contributing Recipe Editors: Mary E. Peterson, Julie H. Turnbull
Test Kitchen Home Economists: Mary Hallin Johnson, Diane Undis
Nutritionists: Elyse A. Cohen, M.S., Nancy Holmes, R.D.
Recipe Copy Editor: Anne Oslund
Editorial Assistant: Joyce Madson
Food Stylists: Kate Courtney, Cindy Lund, Mary Sethre
Photographer: Ed Vetsch
Photography Assistant: Brian Scott Holman
Director, Betty Crocker Food and Publications Center: Marcia Copeland
Assistant Manager, Publications: Lois Tlusty

Seafood Stew with Rosmarina